CONFERENCE OF BISHOPS

OF THE

ANGLICAN COMMUNION

---

*HOLDEN AT LAMBETH PALACE,
JULY 5 TO AUGUST 7, 1920.*

Encyclical Letter

FROM THE BISHOPS,

WITH THE

RESOLUTIONS AND REPORTS.

LONDON
SOCIETY FOR PROMOTING
CHRISTIAN KNOWLEDGE
NEW YORK: THE MACMILLAN COMPANY
1920

CONTENTS

LIST OF BISHOPS ATTENDING THE LAMBETH CONFERENCE OF 1920.

In the arrangement of the following list of Bishops attending the Conference, the general order followed is that of the date of Consecration. In the case of Primates and Metropolitans the order followed, speaking generally, is regulated by the priority of the formation of the Province The Bishops of London, Durham, Winchester, and Meath have an ancient priority which has been recognised in the list.

1 ARCHBISHOP OF CANTERBURY (MOST REV. R T DAVIDSON, D D) 1903. April 25th, 1891.
2 ARCHBISHOP OF YORK (MOST REV C. G LANG, D.D) 1909. May 1st, 1901.
3 ARCHBISHOP OF ARMAGH (MOST REV. C F. D'ARCY, D.D) 1920. February 24th, 1903
4 BISHOP OF CALCUTTA, METROPOLITAN OF INDIA (MOST REV F. WESTCOTT, D.D) 1919. November 30th, 1905.
5 ARCHBISHOP OF SYDNEY (MOST REV J. C. WRIGHT, D D.) 1910. August 24th, 1909
6 ARCHBISHOP OF CAPETOWN (MOST REV W M CARTER, D.D) 1909. September 29th, 1891.
7 ARCHBISHOP OF RUPERT'S LAND (MOST REV. S P. MATHESON, D D) 1905. November 15th, 1903
8 ARCHBISHOP OF THE WEST INDIES AND BISHOP OF GUIANA (MOST REV. E A. PARRY, D D) 1917. December 28th, 1900
9 ARCHBISHOP OF MELBOURNE (MOST REV H LOWTHER CLARKE, D.D.) 1905. November 1st, 1902.
10 ARCHBISHOP OF NOVA SCOTIA (MOST REV C L WORRELL, D D.) 1915. October 18th, 1904.
11 ARCHBISHOP OF BRISBANE (MOST REV. ST C G. A. DONALDSON, D.D) 1905 October 28th, 1904.
12 ARCHBISHOP OF ALGOMA (MOST REV G THORNELOE, D D) 1915 January 6th, 1897.
13 BISHOP OF BRECHIN, PRIMUS OF THE SCOTTISH EPISCOPAL CHURCH (MOST REV. W J F ROBBERDS, D D) 1908. January 6th, 1904.
14 ARCHBISHOP OF WALES (MOST REV A G EDWARDS, D.D) 1920. March 25th, 1889
15 BISHOP OF TENNESSEE (RIGHT REV T F GAILOR, D D) July 25th, 1893.
16 BISHOP OF LONDON (RIGHT REV A F WINNINGTON-INGRAM, D D.) November 30th, 1897.
17 BISHOP OF DURHAM (RIGHT REV. H. HENSLEY HENSON, D D) February 2nd, 1918.

18 BISHOP OF WINCHESTER (RIGHT REV. E. S. TALBOT, D.D.)
                                    October 18th, 1895.
19 BISHOP OF MEATH, PREMIER BISHOP OF IRELAND (MOST REV.
   B. J. PLUNKET, D.D.)   May 13th, 1913.
20 ASSISTANT BISHOP OF BATH AND WELLS (RIGHT REV. W. H.
   STIRLING, D.D.)   December 21st, 1869.
21 ASSISTANT BISHOP FOR TONGA (RIGHT REV. A. WILLIS, D.D.)
                                    February 2nd, 1872.
22 BISHOP R. S. COPLESTON, D.D.   December 28th, 1875.
23 BISHOP OF BATH AND WELLS (RIGHT REV. G. W. KENNION,
   D.D.)   November 30th, 1882.
24 ASSISTANT BISHOP OF WINCHESTER (RIGHT REV. E. G. INGHAM,
   D.D.)   February 24th, 1883.
25 BISHOP OF BETHLEHEM (RIGHT REV. E. TALBOT, D.D.)
                                    May 27th, 1887.
26 BISHOP OF SOUTHERN OHIO (RIGHT REV. BOYD VINCENT, D.D.)
                                    January 25th, 1889.
27 BISHOP H. H. MONTGOMERY, D.D.   May 1st, 1889.
28 BISHOP OF BEVERLEY (RIGHT REV. R. J. CROSTHWAITE, D.D.)
                                    June 11th, 1889.
29 BISHOP OF OHIO (RIGHT REV. W. A. LEONARD, D.D.)
                                    October 12th, 1889.
30 ASSISTANT BISHOP OF ST. ALBANS (RIGHT REV. E. N. HODGES,
   D.D.)   April 25th, 1890.
31 BISHOP OF CHRISTCHURCH (RIGHT REV. C. JULIUS, D.D.)
                                    May 1st, 1890.
32 BISHOP OF WAKEFIELD (RIGHT REV. G. R. EDEN, D.D.)
                                    October 18th, 1890.
33 BISHOP OF COVENTRY (RIGHT REV. H. W. YEATMAN-BIGGS,
   D.D.)   September 29th, 1891.
34 BISHOP OF TEXAS (RIGHT REV. G. H. KINSOLVING, D.D.)
                                    October 12th, 1892.
35 BISHOP OF WILLESDEN (RIGHT REV. W. W. PERRIN, D.D.)
                                    March 25th, 1893.
36 BISHOP (MISSIONARY) OF TOKYO (RIGHT REV. J. McKIM, D.D.)
                                    June 14th, 1893.
37 ASSISTANT BISHOP OF LAGOS (RIGHT REV. I. OLUWOLE, D.D.)
                                    June 29th, 1893.
38 BISHOP OF SASKATCHEWAN (RIGHT REV. J. A. NEWNHAM, D.D.)
                                    August 6th, 1893.
39 ASSISTANT BISHOP OF BIRMINGHAM (RIGHT REV. A. HAMILTON
   BAYNES, D.D.)   September 29th, 1893.
40 BISHOP OF MASSACHUSETTS (RIGHT REV. W. LAWRENCE, D.D.)
                                    October 5th, 1893.
41 BISHOP OF NORTH CAROLINA (RIGHT REV. J. B. CHESHIRE, D.D.)
                                    October 15th, 1893.
42 BISHOP OF VERMONT (RIGHT REV. A. C. A. HALL, D.D.)
                                    February 2nd, 1894.
43 BISHOP OF BUNBURY (RIGHT REV. C. WILSON, D.D.)
                                    June 11th, 1894.
44 BISHOP OF MANCHESTER (RIGHT REV. E. A. KNOX, D.D.)
                                    December 28th, 1894.
45 BISHOP G. F. BROWNE, D.D.   April 21st, 1895.

46 BISHOP OF ROCHESTER (RIGHT REV. J. R. HARMER, D.D.)
May 23rd, 1895.
47 BISHOP OF RIVERINA (RIGHT REV. E. A. ANDERSON, D.D.)
June 29th, 1895.
48 BISHOP OF WESTERN CHINA (RIGHT REV. W. W. CASSELS, D.D.)
October 18th, 1895
49 BISHOP G. MOTT WILLIAMS, D.D.   May 1st, 1896.
50 BISHOP OF GRANTHAM (RIGHT REV. J. E. HINE, D.D.)
June 29th, 1896.
51 BISHOP OF CREDITON (RIGHT REV. R. E. TREFUSIS, D.D.)
February 24th, 1897.
52 BISHOP OF ST. DAVID'S (RIGHT REV. J. OWEN, D.D.)
May 1st, 1897.
53 BISHOP OF CONNECTICUT (RIGHT REV. C. B. BREWSTER, D.D.)
October 28th, 1897.
54 BISHOP OF SOUTHAMPTON (RIGHT REV. J. MACARTHUR, D.D.)
September 29th, 1898.
55 BISHOP (MISSIONARY) OF ASHEVILLE (RIGHT REV. J. M. HORNER,
D.D.)   December 28th, 1898.
56 BISHOP (MISSIONARY) OF SOUTHERN BRAZIL (RIGHT REV. L. L.
KINSOLVING, D.D.)   January 6th, 1899.
57 BISHOP OF SACRAMENTO (RIGHT REV. W. H. MORELAND, D.D.)
January 25th, 1899
58 BISHOP OF BANGOR (RIGHT REV. W. H. WILLIAMS, D.D.)
February 2nd, 1899.
59 BISHOP OF OSAKA (RIGHT REV. H. J. FOSS, D.D.)
February 2nd, 1899.
60 BISHOP OF MADRAS (RIGHT REV. H. WHITEHEAD, D.D.)
June 29th, 1899.
61 BISHOP G. L. KING, D.D.   June 29th, 1899.
62 BISHOP OF WEST VIRGINIA (RIGHT REV. W. L. GRAVATT, D.D.)
November 10th, 1899.
63 BISHOP OF WEST MISSOURI (RIGHT REV. S. C. PARTRIDGE, D.D.)
February 2nd, 1900.
64 BISHOP OF LIVERPOOL (RIGHT REV. F. J. CHAVASSE, D.D.)
April 25th, 1900.
65 BISHOP OF WILLOCHRA (RIGHT REV. G. WHITE, D.D.)
August 24th, 1900.
66 BISHOP OF SALISBURY (RIGHT REV. F. E. RIDGEWAY, D.D.)
February 17th, 1901.
67 BISHOP OF NATAL (RIGHT REV. F. S. BAINES, D.D.)
August 4th, 1901.
68 BISHOP OF JARROW (RIGHT REV. J. N. QUIRK, D.D.)
October 18th, 1901.
69 BISHOP OF SOUTHWELL (RIGHT REV. E. HOSKYNS, D.D.)
October 18th, 1901.
70 BISHOP OF ST. JOHN'S, KAFFRARIA (RIGHT REV. J. W. WILLIAMS,
D.D.)   November 30th, 1901.
71 BISHOP (MISSIONARY) OF SOUTHERN FLORIDA (RIGHT REV. C.
MANN, D.D.)   December 4th, 1901.
72 BISHOP OF WESTERN NEW YORK (RIGHT REV. C. H. BRENT,
D.D.)   December 19th, 1901.
73 BISHOP (MISSIONARY) OF OLYMPIA (RIGHT REV. F. W. KEATOR,
D.D.)   January 8th, 1902.

74 Bishop of Long Island (Right Rev. F. Burgess, D.D.)
            January 15th, 1902.
75 Bishop of North-West Australia (Right Rev. G. Trower,
  D.D.)   January 25th, 1902.
76 Bishop in Argentina (Right Rev. E. F. Every, D D.)
             July 14th, 1902.
77 Bishop of Nagpur (Right Rev. E. Chatterton, D.D.)
            March 25th, 1903.
78 Bishop of Zululand (Right Rev. W. L. Vyvyan, D D.)
             May 21st, 1903.
79 Bishop of Thetford (Right Rev. J. P. A. Bowers, D D.)
             June 29th, 1903.
80 Bishop of Colombo (Right Rev. E A Copleston, D D.)
            August 30th, 1903
81 Bishop of Shantung (Right Rev. G. D. Iliff, D.D.)
           October 28th, 1903.
82 Bishop of Newark (Right Rev. E S. Lines, D.D.)
          November 18th, 1903.
83 Bishop of Croydon (Right Rev H. H. Pereira, D.D.)
           January 25th, 1904.
84 Bishop of Glasgow (Right Rev. A. E. Campbell, D.D.)
           February 24th, 1904.
85 Bishop E. W. Osborne, D.D.   October 23rd, 1904.
86 Bishop (Missionary) of Hankow (Right Rev. L. H. Roots,
  D.D)   November 14th, 1904.
87 Bishop of Moray, Ross, and Caithness (Right Rev. A. J.
  Maclean, D.D)   December 21st, 1904.
88 Bishop of Huron (Right Rev D Williams, D D.)
            January 6th, 1905.
89 Bishop in South Tokyo (Right Rev. C. H. Boutflower, D.D.)
           January 25th, 1905.
90 Bishop of Harrisburg (Right Rev. J. H. Darlington, D D.)
            April 26th, 1905.
91 Bishop of Gloucester (Right Rev. E. C S. Gibson, D D)
             June 1st, 1905.
92 Bishop of Llandaff (Right Rev. J. P. Hughes, D.D.)
             June 1st, 1905.
93 Bishop of St. Helena (Right Rev. W. A Holbech, D D.)
94 Bishop of Ely (Right Rev F H Chase, D D.) June 24th, 1905
           October 18th, 1905.
95 Assistant Bishop of Salisbury (Right Rev. A E. Joscelyne,
  D D)   October 18th, 1905.
96 Coadjutor Bishop of Missouri (Right Rev. F. F. Johnson,
  D.D.)   November 2nd, 1905.
97 Bishop of Knaresborough (Right Rev. L. F. M B Smith,
  D D.)   December 27th, 1905.
98 Bishop of Adelaide (Right Rev. A. Nutter Thomas, D D.)
           February 2nd, 1906.
99 Assistant Bishop of Ely (Right Rev. H. M. E. Price, D.D)
           February 2nd, 1906.
100 Bishop of Michigan (Right Rev. C. D Williams, D D.)
           February 7th, 1906.
101 Bishop of Western Michigan (Right Rev. J. N. McCormick,
  D.D.)   February 14th, 1906.

102 BISHOP OF MILWAUKEE (RIGHT REV. W. W. WEBB, D.D.)
February 24th, 1906.

103 BISHOP OF CHESTER (RIGHT REV. H. L. PAGET, D.D.)
April 25th, 1906.

104 BISHOP OF BRISTOL (RIGHT REV. G. NICKSON, D.D.)
June 29th, 1906.

105 BISHOP OF FREDERICTON (RIGHT REV. J. A. RICHARDSON, D.D.)
November 30th, 1906.

106 BISHOP OF ARGYLL AND THE ISLES (RIGHT REV. K. MAC-
KENZIE, D.D.) January 25th, 1907.

107 BISHOP OF SOUTH CAROLINA (RIGHT REV. W. A GUERRY, D.D.)
September 15th, 1907.

108 BISHOP IN CHEKIANG (RIGHT REV. H. J. MOLONY, D.D.)
January 25th, 1908.

109 BISHOP OF CLOGHER (RIGHT REV. M. DAY, D.D.)
January 25th, 1908.

110 BISHOP OF ST. ANDREWS, DUNKELD, AND DUNBLANE (RIGHT
REV. C. E. PLUMB, D.D.) March 25th, 1908.

111 BISHOP OF BOMBAY (RIGHT REV. E. J. PALMER, D.D.)
May 28th, 1908.

112 BISHOP IN POLYNESIA (RIGHT REV. T. C. TWITCHELL, D.D.)
May 28th, 1908.

113 BISHOP IN KHARTOUM (RIGHT REV. Ll H. GWYNNE, D.D.)
October 11th, 1908.

114 BISHOP OF ZANZIBAR (RIGHT REV. F. WESTON, D.D.)
October 11th, 1908.

115 BISHOP OF MONTREAL (RIGHT REV. J. C. FARTHING, D.D.)
January 6th, 1909.

116 BISHOP OF WASHINGTON (RIGHT REV. A. HARDING, D.D.)
January 25th, 1909.

117 BISHOP OF COLCHESTER (RIGHT REV. R. H. WHITCOMBE, D.D.)
February 2nd, 1909.

118 BISHOP OF ROCKHAMPTON (RIGHT REV. G. D. HALFORD, D.D.)
February 2nd, 1909.

119 BISHOP OF GUILDFORD (RIGHT REV. J. H. G. RANDOLPH, D.D.)
February 21st, 1909.

120 BISHOP OF TORONTO (RIGHT REV. J. F. SWEENY, D.D.)
March 25th, 1909.

121 BISHOP (MISSIONARY) OF WYOMING (RIGHT REV. N. S. THOMAS,
D.D.) May 6th, 1909.

122 BISHOP OF MOOSONEE (RIGHT REV. J. G ANDERSON, D.D.)
May 16th, 1909

123 BISHOP OF MAINE (RIGHT REV. B. BREWSTER, D.D.)
June 17th, 1909.

124 BISHOP OF ST. ALBANS (RIGHT REV M. B. FURSE, D.D.)
June 29th, 1909.

125 BISHOP OF BURNLEY (RIGHT REV. H. HENN, D.D.)
July 11th, 1909.

126 BISHOP OF SHEFFIELD (RIGHT REV. L. H. BURROWS, D.D.)
July 11th, 1909.

127 BISHOP OF SINGAPORE (RIGHT REV. C. J. FERGUSON-DAVIE,
D.D.) August 24th, 1909.

128 BISHOP OF BARROW (RIGHT REV. C. WEST WATSON, D.D.)
September 21st, 1909.

129 BISHOP OF WHALLEY (RIGHT REV A. G RAWSTORNE, D D)
            September 21st, 1909.
130 BISHOP OF MARYLAND (RIGHT REV J G. MURRAY, D D)
            September 29th, 1909.
131 BISHOP OF DERBY (RIGHT REV. C. T ABRAHAM, D D)
            November 30th, 1909.
132 BISHOP OF HONAN (RIGHT REV W C WHITE, D.D)
            November 30th, 1909
133 BISHOP IN KWANGSI AND HUNAN (RIGHT REV. W. BANISTER,
            D D)   November 30th, 1909
134 BISHOP IN KYUSHU, SOUTH JAPAN (RIGHT REV. A LEA, D D)
            November 30th, 1909.
135 BISHOP OF AUCKLAND (RIGHT REV. A W. AVERILL, D D.
            January 16th, 1910
136 BISHOP OF RANGOON (RIGHT REV. R. S FYFFE, D D)
            January 16th, 1910
137 BISHOP OF NEW GUINEA (RIGHT REV G SHARP, D D)
            April 25th, 1910
138 BISHOP OF NORWICH (RIGHT REV. B POLLOCK, D.D.)
            April 25th, 1910.
139 BISHOP OF LICHFIELD (RIGHT REV. J A. KEMPTHORNE, D D.)
            May 16th, 1910.
140 BISHOP OF EDINBURGH (RIGHT REV. G. H. S. WALPOLE, D D.)
            June 24th, 1910.
141 BISHOP OF NYASALAND (RIGHT REV. T. C. FISHER, D D)
            June 24th, 1910
142 BISHOP OF SIERRA LEONE (RIGHT REV J WALMSLEY, D.D.)
            June 24th, 1910
143 BISHOP OF NEW WESTMINSTER (RIGHT REV. A U DE PENCIER,
            D D)   July 25th, 1910.
144 BISHOP OF LUCKNOW (RIGHT REV G. H WESTCOTT, D D.)
            November 6th, 1910.
145 BISHOP (MISSIONARY) OF WESTERN NEBRASKA (RIGHT REV.
            G A. BEECHER, D.D.)   November 30th, 1910.
146 BISHOP (MISSIONARY) OF NORTH TEXAS (RIGHT REV E A.
            TEMPLE, D D)   December 15th, 1910.
147 ASSISTANT BISHOP OF BLOEMFONTEIN (RIGHT REV. F R T
            BALFOUR, M A)   January 1st, 1911.
148 BISHOP OF SOUTHERN RHODESIA (RIGHT REV F H BEAVEN,
            D.D)   January 1st, 1911.
149 BISHOP OF RHODE ISLAND (RIGHT REV J D PERRY, D D)
            January 6th, 1911.
150 BISHOP OF ANTIGUA (RIGHT REV E HUTSON, D D)
            January 15th, 1911.
151 BISHOP (MISSIONARY) OF ARIZONA (RIGHT REV J W ATWOOD,
            D.D.)   January 18th, 1911.
152 BISHOP (MISSIONARY) OF OKLAHOMA (RIGHT REV. T P.
            THURSTON, D D.)   January 25th, 1911
153 BISHOP OF NEW YORK (RIGHT REV C. S. BURCH, D.D.)
            February 24th, 1911.
154 ASSISTANT BISHOP OF LLANDAFF (RIGHT REV O T L CROSSLEY,
            D D)   April 25th, 1911.
155 BISHOP OF OXFORD (RIGHT REV. H. M. BURGE, D.D.)
            May 25th, 1911.

156 BISHOP IN COREA (RIGHT REV M. N. TROLLOPE, D D)
July 25th, 1911

157 BISHOP OF GIBRALTAR (RIGHT REV. H. J. C KNIGHT, D D)
July 25th, 1911

158 BISHOP OF TAUNTON (RIGHT REV. C F DE SALIS, D.D)
July 25th, 1911

159 BISHOP OF GRAFTON (RIGHT REV. C. H. DRUITT, D D)
August 6th, 1911

160 BISHOP OF GEORGE (RIGHT REV H. B. SIDWELL, D. D.)
September 29th, 1911

161 BISHOP OF WESTERN MASSACHUSETTS (RIGHT REV T. F DAVIES, D.D.)
October 18th, 1911

162 BISHOP OF BIRMINGHAM (RIGHT REV. H R WAKEFIELD, D D)
October 28th, 1911

163 BISHOP OF PENNSYLVANIA (RIGHT REV. P M RHINELANDER, D D)
October 28th, 1911

164 SUFFRAGAN BISHOP OF PENNSYLVANIA (RIGHT REV T. J. GARLAND, D.D.)
October 28th, 1911

165 BISHOP OF KENSINGTON (RIGHT REV. J. P MAUD, D.D.)
December 28th, 1911.

166 BISHOP OF UGANDA (RIGHT REV. J J WILLIS, D D)
January 25th, 1912.

167 BISHOP OF OTTAWA (RIGHT REV. J C ROPER, D D)
February 24th, 1912

168 BISHOP OF SODOR AND MAN (RIGHT REV. J D THOMPSON, D D)
March 25th, 1912.

169 BISHOP OF CORK, CLOYNE, AND ROSS (RIGHT REV C B DOWSE, D.D)
June 11th, 1912

170 BISHOP OF KIMBERLEY AND KURUMAN (RIGHT REV. W GORE-BROWNE, M A.)
June 29th, 1912

171 BISHOP OF CHICHESTER (RIGHT REV W O BURROWS, D D)
July 25th, 1912.

172 BISHOP OF ATHABASCA (RIGHT REV. E F ROBINS, D.D.)
November 24th, 1912

173 BISHOP OF DORNAKAL (RIGHT REV V S AZARIAH, D D)
December 29th, 1912.

174 BISHOP OF ACCRA (RIGHT REV. M S O'RORKE, D D)
January 25th, 1913

175 ASSISTANT BISHOP OF NATAL (RIGHT REV. F. ROACH, D D)
January 25th, 1913

176 BISHOP OF NORTH QUEENSLAND (RIGHT REV J O FEETHAM, D D)
April 25th, 1913

177 BISHOP OF LEICESTER (RIGHT REV. N. McL LANG, D D)
May 1st, 1913

178 BISHOP OF ONTARIO (RIGHT REV. E. J. BIDWELL, D D)
June 24th, 1913

179 BISHOP OF MACKENZIE RIVER (RIGHT REV. J. R. LUCAS, D.D)
August 31st, 1913

180 BISHOP OF HULL (RIGHT REV F. GURDON, D.D)
September 29th, 1913

181 BISHOP OF RICHMOND (RIGHT REV. F. C. KILNER, D D)
September 29th, 1913.

182 BISHOP OF JAMAICA (RIGHT REV. G. F C DE CARTERET, D D)
October 18th, 1913.

183 BISHOP OF BUCKINGHAM (RIGHT REV E D. SHAW, D.D.)
January 1st, 1914.

184 BISHOP IN NORTH CHINA (RIGHT REV F. L. NORRIS, D.D.)
January 1st, 1914.

185 COADJUTOR BISHOP OF OHIO (RIGHT REV. F. DU MOULIN, D D)
January 8th, 1914.

186 BISHOP (MISSIONARY) OF NEW MEXICO (RIGHT REV F B.
HOWDEN, D.D.)   January 14th, 1914.

187 BISHOP OF WAIAPU (RIGHT REV. W W SEDGWICK, D D)
February 22nd, 1914.

188 BISHOP OF CHELMSFORD (RIGHT REV J E WATTS-DITCHFIELD,
D D)   February 24th, 1914.

189 BISHOP OF ST EDMUNDSBURY AND IPSWICH (RIGHT REV. H B
HODGSON, D D)   February 24th, 1914.

190 BISHOP OF EDMONTON (RIGHT REV. H A GRAY, D D.)
March 25th, 1914.

191 BISHOP OF NORTHERN RHODESIA (RIGHT REV A J. W MAY,
D D)   April 25th, 1914

192 BISHOP OF NEWCASTLE, N.S.W. (RIGHT REV R STEPHEN, D D.)
September 13th, 1914.

193 BISHOP IN JERUSALEM (RIGHT REV R. MACINNES, D.D.)
October 28th, 1914.

194 BISHOP OF VIRGINIA (RIGHT REV. W. C. BROWN, D.D.)
October 28th, 1914.

195 BISHOP OF KINGSTON-ON-THAMES (RIGHT REV S. M TAYLOR,
D.D.)   January 6th, 1915.

196 BISHOP IN ASSAM (RIGHT REV H PAKENHAM-WALSH, D D)
January 10th, 1915

197 BISHOP OF NEW JERSEY (RIGHT REV P MATTHEWS, D.D.)
January 25th, 1915.

198 BISHOP OF QUEBEC (RIGHT REV. L W WILLIAMS, D D)
January 25th, 1915.

199 BISHOP OF KOOTENAY (RIGHT REV. A J DOULL, D D)
February 24th, 1915

200 BISHOP OF GOULBURN (RIGHT REV L B RADFORD, D.D.)
August 24th, 1915.

201 BISHOP OF CARPENTARIA (RIGHT REV. H NEWTON, D D)
September 21st, 1915.

202 BISHOP OF STAFFORD (RIGHT REV. L P CRAWFURD, D.D.)
September 29th, 1915.

203 BISHOP OF SWANSEA (RIGHT REV. E L BEVAN, D D)
September 30th, 1915.

204 COADJUTOR BISHOP OF NEWARK (RIGHT REV. W. R STEARLY,
D D)   October 21st, 1915

205 BISHOP OF GRAHAMSTOWN (RIGHT REV F R PHELPS, D.D.)
October 31st, 1915

206 BISHOP IN TINNEVELLY AND MADURA (RIGHT REV. E. H. M.
WALLER, D D)   November 28th, 1915

207 BISHOP OF KILMORE, ELPHIN, AND ARDAGH (RIGHT REV. W R
MOORE, D D)   November 30th, 1915

208 BISHOP OF NEWCASTLE (RIGHT REV. H L WILD, D D)
November 30th, 1915.

209 BISHOP OF OSSORY, FERNS, AND LEIGHLIN (RIGHT REV. J A. F.
GREGG, D D)   December 28th, 1915.

210 BISHOP OF DOVER (RIGHT REV. H E. BILBROUGH, D.D)
February 24th, 1916

211 BISHOP OF DERRY AND RAPHOE (RIGHT REV. J. I. PEACOCKE,
D.D.)   April 25th, 1916.

212 BISHOP OF PETERBOROUGH (RIGHT REV. F. T Woods, D.D.)
September 21st, 1916.

213 BISHOP OF KANSAS (RIGHT REV. J. WISE, D D.)
October 28th, 1916.

214 BISHOP OF COLUMBIA (RIGHT REV C DE V SCHOFIELD, D D)
November 30th, 1916

215 BISHOP (MISSIONARY) OF SOUTH DAKOTA (RIGHT REV H L
BURLESON, D D)   December 14th, 1916.

216 BISHOP OF EXETER (RIGHT REV THE LORD WILLIAM CECIL,
D D)   December 28th, 1916

217 BISHOP OF BALLARAT (RIGHT REV. M. H. MAXWELL-GUMBLETON,
D D)   January 1st, 1917.

218 BISHOP OF ABERDEEN AND ORKNEY (RIGHT REV. F L. DEANE,
D D)   May 1st, 1917.

219 COADJUTOR BISHOP OF CAPETOWN (RIGHT REV J O. NASH,
D D)   May 17th, 1917

220 BISHOP OF BARBADOS (RIGHT REV. A. P. BERKELEY, D D.)
August 12th, 1917.

221 BISHOP OF HONDURAS (BRITISH) (RIGHT REV. E. A. DUNN,
D D)   August 12th, 1917

222 BISHOP OF ATLANTA (RIGHT REV. H. J. MIKELL, D.D.)
November 1st, 1917

223 BISHOP OF GIPPSLAND (RIGHT REV. G H. CRANSWICK, D D)
November 1st, 1917

224 SUFFRAGAN BISHOP OF SOUTH DAKOTA (RIGHT REV. W. P.
REMINGTON, D D)   January 10th, 1918.

225 BISHOP OF WOOLWICH (RIGHT REV. W W. HOUGH, D D.)
February 2nd, 1918

226 BISHOP OF NEWFOUNDLAND (RIGHT REV W. C WHITE, D D)
March 10th, 1918

227 BISHOP OF MOMBASA (RIGHT REV. R. S. HEYWOOD, M A.)
April 21st, 1918

228 BISHOP IN FUKIEN (RIGHT REV. J HIND, D.D.)
October 18th, 1918

229 BISHOP OF WARRINGTON (RIGHT REV M LINTON SMITH, D D.)
November 1st, 1918

230 BISHOP OF WORCESTER (RIGHT REV. E. H PEARCE, LITT.D.)
February 24th, 1919.

231 BISHOP OF CASHEL (RIGHT REV. R MILLER, D D.)
June 11th, 1919

232 BISHOP OF THE FALKLAND ISLES (RIGHT REV N. S DE JERSEY,
D.D.)   June 24th, 1919

233 BISHOP OF NASSAU (RIGHT REV. R G. SHEDDEN, D D.)
June 24th, 1919.

234 BISHOP OF BARKING (RIGHT REV. J. T. INSKIP, D D)
June 24th, 1919.

235 BISHOP OF TASMANIA (RIGHT REV R S. HAY, D D)
August 24th, 1919.

236 BISHOP OF NEBRASKA (RIGHT REV. E. V SHAYLER, D D)
September 11th, 1919

237 BISHOP OF TRURO (RIGHT REV. F. S. G WARMAN, D.D.)
                                    October 18th, 1919.
238 BISHOP OF SOUTHWARK (RIGHT REV. C. F. GARBETT, D D)
                                    October 18th, 1919.
239 BISHOP OF STEPNEY (RIGHT REV H. MOSLEY, D D.)
                                    October 18th, 1919
240 BISHOP OF LAGOS (RIGHT REV. F. MELVILLE JONES, D.D.)
                                    October 18th, 1919
241 BISHOP IN PERSIA (RIGHT REV J H LINTON, D.D.)
                                    October 18th, 1919.
242 BISHOP OF DOWN (RIGHT REV. C. T. P. GRIERSON, D D)
                                    October 28th, 1919
243 BISHOP OF KALGOORLIE (RIGHT REV. W. E. ELSEY, M.A.)
                                    November 9th, 1919.
244 BISHOP OF LINCOLN (RIGHT REV. W S. SWAYNE, D D)
                                    January 6th, 1920.
245 BISHOP OF BENDIGO (RIGHT REV D. BAKER, D D)
                                    February 2nd, 1920
246 BISHOP OF BRADFORD (RIGHT REV A W T. PEROWNE, D D)
                                    February 2nd, 1920
247 BISHOP OF TUAM (RIGHT REV. A E ROSS, D D)
                                    February 24th, 1920.
248 BISHOP OF PRETORIA (RIGHT REV N S. TALBOT, D D)
                                    June 24th, 1920
249 BISHOP OF VICTORIA, HONGKONG (RIGHT REV. C R DUPPUY,
        M.A)   June 24th, 1920.
250 SUFFRAGAN BISHOP OF LEWES (RIGHT REV. H K. SOUTHWELL,
        M A.)   June 24th, 1920
251 ASSISTANT BISHOP IN WESTERN EQUATORIAL AFRICA (RIGHT
        REV. A. W. HOWELLS, M A)   June 24th, 1920.
252 BISHOP OF KAMPALA (RIGHT REV H GRESFORD JONES, D D)
                                    June 24th, 1920.

LIST OF BISHOPS ATTENDING THE LAMBETH CONFERENCE OF 1920, ARRANGED ACCORDING TO PROVINCES.

ARCHBISHOP OF CANTERBURY (MOST REV R. T. DAVIDSON, D D.).
  BISHOP OF DOVER (RT REV. H. E. BILBROUGH, D.D.).
  BISHOP OF CROYDON (RT REV. H. H. PEREIRA, D D.)
BISHOP OF LONDON (RT. REV. A. F. WINNINGTON-INGRAM, D.D.).
  BISHOP OF STEPNEY (RT. REV H MOSLEY, D D.)
  BISHOP OF KENSINGTON (RT. REV. J. P. MAUD, D.D.).
  BISHOP OF WILLESDEN (RT. REV W. W. PERRIN, D D)
BISHOP OF WINCHESTER (RT. REV. E. S TALBOT, D.D.)
  BISHOP OF SOUTHAMPTON (RT. REV. J. MACARTHUR, D.D.)
  BISHOP OF GUILDFORD (RT. REV. J. H. G. RANDOLPH, D D.).
  ASSISTANT BISHOP OF WINCHESTER (RT. REV. E. G INGHAM, D D)
BISHOP OF BATH AND WELLS (RT. REV. G. W. KENNION, D.D.).
  BISHOP OF TAUNTON (RT. REV. C. F. DE SALIS, D.D.)
  ASSISTANT BISHOP OF BATH AND WELLS (RT REV. W. H STIRLING, D.D.).
BISHOP OF BIRMINGHAM (RT REV H R WAKEFIELD, D.D.)
  ASSISTANT BISHOP OF BIRMINGHAM (RT. REV. A. HAMILTON BAYNES, D.D.).
BISHOP OF BRISTOL (RT. REV. G. NICKSON, D.D.).
BISHOP OF CHELMSFORD (RT. REV. J. E. WATTS-DITCHFIELD, D.D.).
  BISHOP OF BARKING (RT. REV. J. T. INSKIP, D.D.).
  BISHOP OF COLCHESTER (RT. REV. R H. WHITCOMBE, D D.).
BISHOP OF CHICHESTER (RT. REV. W. O. BURROWS, D.D.).
  BISHOP OF LEWES (RT. REV H. K. SOUTHWELL, M.A)
BISHOP OF COVENTRY (RT. REV H W. YEATMAN-BIGGS, D D.).
BISHOP OF ELY (RT. REV. F. H. CHASE, D.D.).
  ASSISTANT BISHOP OF ELY (RT. REV. H. M. E. PRICE, D.D.).
BISHOP OF EXETER (RT REV LORD WILLIAM CECIL, D.D.).
  BISHOP OF CREDITON (RT. REV R. E. TREFUSIS, D.D)
BISHOP OF GLOUCESTER (RT REV E C. S. GIBSON, D.D).
BISHOP OF LICHFIELD (RT. REV J A. KEMPTHORNE, D.D.).
  BISHOP OF STAFFORD (RT. REV. L. P. CRAWFURD, D.D.)
BISHOP OF LINCOLN (RT. REV. W S. SWAYNE, D.D.)
  BISHOP OF GRANTHAM (RT. REV J. E HINE, D D.).
BISHOP OF NORWICH (RT. REV. B POLLOCK, D.D.).
  BISHOP OF THETFORD (RT. REV. J P. A BOWERS, D D.).
BISHOP OF OXFORD (RT. REV. H. M. BURGE, D.D.).
  BISHOP OF BUCKINGHAM (RT REV. E. D. SHAW, D.D).
BISHOP OF PETERBOROUGH (RT. REV F. T. WOODS, D.D.).
  BISHOP OF LEICESTER (RT. REV. N. MCL. LANG, D D.)
BISHOP OF ROCHESTER (RT. REV J R HARMER, D.D.).
BISHOP OF ST ALBANS (RT. REV M. B. FURSE, D D.).
  ASSISTANT BISHOP OF ST. ALBANS (RT. REV. E N. HODGES, D.D.).

BISHOP OF ST. EDMUNDSBURY AND IPSWICH (RT. REV. H. B.
    HODGSON, D.D.)
BISHOP OF SALISBURY (RT. REV. F. E. RIDGEWAY, D.D.).
    ASSISTANT BISHOP OF SALISBURY (RT. REV. A. E. JOSCELYNE,
      D.D.).
BISHOP OF SOUTHWARK (RT. REV. C. F. GARBETT, D.D.).
    BISHOP OF KINGSTON-ON-THAMES (RT. REV. S. M. TAYLOR,
      D.D.).
    BISHOP OF WOOLWICH (RT. REV. W. W. HOUGH, D.D.).
BISHOP OF SOUTHWELL (RT. REV. E. HOSKYNS, D.D.).
    BISHOP OF DERBY (RT. REV. C. T. ABRAHAM, D.D.).
BISHOP OF TRURO (RT. REV. F. S. G. WARMAN, D.D.)
BISHOP OF WORCESTER (RT. REV. E. H. PEARCE, LITT.D.)
RT. REV. G. F. BROWNE, D.D.
RT. REV. R. S. COPLESTON, D.D.
RT. REV. G. L. KING, D.D.
RT. REV. H. H. MONTGOMERY, D.D.

ARCHBISHOP OF YORK (MOST REV. C. G. LANG, D.D.)
    BISHOP OF BEVERLEY (RT. REV. R. J. CROSTHWAITE, D.D.)
    BISHOP OF HULL (RT. REV. F. GURDON, D.D.).
BISHOP OF DURHAM (RT. REV. H. HENSLEY HENSON, D.D.).
    BISHOP OF JARROW (RT. REV. J. N. QUIRK, D.D.)
BISHOP OF BRADFORD (RT. REV. A. W. T. PEROWNE, D.D.)
[BISHOP OF CARLISLE]
    BISHOP OF BARROW (RT. REV. C. WEST WATSON, D.D.).
BISHOP OF CHESTER (RT. REV. H. L. PAGET, D.D.)
BISHOP OF LIVERPOOL (RT. REV. F. J. CHAVASSE, D.D.).
    BISHOP OF WARRINGTON (RT. REV. M. LINTON SMITH, D.D.).
BISHOP OF MANCHESTER (RT. REV. E. A. KNOX, D.D.).
    BISHOP OF BURNLEY (RT. REV. H. HENN, D.D.)
    BISHOP OF WHALLEY (RT. REV. A. G. RAWSTORNE, D.D.).
BISHOP OF NEWCASTLE (RT. REV. H. L. WILD, D.D.)
[BISHOP OF RIPON]
    BISHOP OF KNARESBOROUGH (RT. REV. L. F. M. B. SMITH, D.D.)
    BISHOP OF RICHMOND (F. C. KILNER, D.D.).
BISHOP OF SHEFFIELD (RT. REV. L. H. BURROWS, D.D.).
BISHOP OF SODOR AND MAN (RT. REV. J. DENTON THOMPSON, D.D.).
BISHOP OF WAKEFIELD (RT. REV. G. R. EDEN, D.D.).

ARCHBISHOP OF ARMAGH (MOST REV. C. F. D'ARCY, D.D.).
BISHOP OF MEATH (MOST REV. B. J. PLUNKET, D.D.)
BISHOP OF CLOGHER (RT. REV. M. DAY, D.D.).
BISHOP OF DERRY AND RAPHOE (RT. REV. J. I. PEACOCKE, D.D.)
BISHOP OF DOWN, CONNOR AND DROMORE (RT. REV. C. T. P. GRIER-
    SON, D.D.)
BISHOP OF KILMORE, ELPHIN AND ARDAGH (RT. REV. W. R. MOORE,
    D.D.)
BISHOP OF TUAM, KILLALA AND ACHONRY (RT. REV. A. E. ROSS,
    D.D.)

BISHOP OF CASHEL, EMLY, WATERFORD AND LISMORE (RT. REV. R.
    MILLER, D.D.).

BISHOP OF CORK, CLOYNE AND ROSS (RT. REV. C. B DOWSE, D.D.).
BISHOP OF OSSORY, FERNS AND LEIGHLIN (RT. REV. J. A. F. GREGG, D.D.).

ARCHBISHOP OF WALES (MOST REV. E. G. EDWARDS, D D)
BISHOP OF BANGOR (RT REV. W. H. WILLIAMS, D.D.).
BISHOP OF LLANDAFF (RT. REV. J. P. HUGHES, D D.).
    ASSISTANT BISHOP OF LLANDAFF (RT. REV. O. T. L. CROSSLEY, D D).
BISHOP OF ST DAVIDS (RT REV J OWEN, D D).
    BISHOP OF SWANSEA (RT REV. E. L. BEVAN, D.D.).

BISHOP OF BRECHIN, *Primus* (MOST REV. W. J. F. ROBBERDS, D.D).
BISHOP OF ABERDEEN (RT. REV F. L. DEANE, D.D)
BISHOP OF ARGYLL (RT REV. K. MACKENZIE, D D.).
BISHOP OF EDINBURGH (RT. REV. G. H S WALPOLE, D D)
BISHOP OF GLASGOW AND GALLOWAY (RT. REV. A. E. CAMPBELL, D D)
BISHOP OF MORAY, ROSS, AND CAITHNESS (RT. REV. A. J. MACLEAN, D.D.).
BISHOP OF ST. ANDREWS, DUNKELD, AND DUNBLANE (RT. REV. C. E. PLUMB, D.D.).

BISHOP OF CALCUTTA, *Metropolitan* (MOST REV. F WESTCOTT, D.D).
BISHOP IN ASSAM (RT REV. H PAKENHAM-WALSH, D.D.).
BISHOP OF BOMBAY (RT REV. J PALMER, D D)
BISHOP OF COLOMBO (RT. REV. E. A. COPLESTON, D.D.).
BISHOP OF DORNAKAL (RT. REV. V. S. AZARIAH, D.D.).
BISHOP OF LUCKNOW (RT. REV G H. WESTCOTT, D.D.).
BISHOP OF MADRAS (RT. REV. H. WHITEHEAD, D D.).
BISHOP OF NAGPUR (RT. REV. E. CHATTERTON, D D).
BISHOP OF RANGOON (RT. REV. R. S FYFFE, D D).
BISHOP IN TINNEVELLY AND MADURA (RT. REV. E. H. M. WALLER, D.D.).

ARCHBISHOP OF CAPETOWN, *Metropolitan* (MOST REV. W. M. CARTER, D D).
    COADJUTOR BISHOP OF CAPETOWN (RT. REV. J. O. NASH, D.D.).
[BISHOP OF BLOEMFONTEIN.]
    ASSISTANT BISHOP OF BLOEMFONTEIN (RT REV. F. R. T. BALFOUR, M.A)
BISHOP OF GEORGE (RT REV. H B SIDWELL, D D.).
BISHOP OF GRAHAMSTOWN (RT. REV. F. R. PHELPS, D D)
BISHOP OF KIMBERLEY AND KURUMAN (RT REV W. GORE-BROWNE, M.A.).
BISHOP OF NATAL (RT. REV. F. S BAINES, D D.).
    ASSISTANT BISHOP OF NATAL (RT. REV. F. ROACH, D.D.).
BISHOP OF PRETORIA (RT. REV N S TALBOT, D.D).
BISHOP OF SOUTHERN RHODESIA (RT. REV. F H BEAVEN, D D.).
BISHOP OF ST. HELENA (RT. REV. W A. HOLBECH, D.D.).
BISHOP OF ST. JOHN'S, KAFFRARIA (RT REV. J. W. WILLIAMS, D.D).
BISHOP OF ZULULAND (RT REV. W L. VYVYAN, D.D).

ARCHBISHOP OF RUPERT'S LAND, *Primate and Metropolitan* (MOST
　　REV S P MATHESON, D.D.).
BISHOP OF ATHABASCA (RT. REV. E. F ROBINS, D D.).
BISHOP OF EDMONTON (RT. REV. H A GRAY, D D.).
BISHOP OF HONAN (RT REV. W. C WHITE, D.D).
BISHOP OF MACKENZIE RIVER (RT REV. J R. LUCAS, D.D)
BISHOP OF MOOSONEE (RT. REV. J G ANDERSON, D.D.)
BISHOP OF SASKATCHEWAN (RT REV J A NEWNHAM, D.D.)

ARCHBISHOP OF NOVA SCOTIA, *Metropolitan* (MOST REV. C. L.
　　WORRELL, D D)
BISHOP OF FREDERICTON (RT REV. J. A. RICHARDSON, D D).
BISHOP OF MONTREAL (RT REV J C FARTHING, D D.).
BISHOP OF QUEBEC (RT REV L W WILLIAMS. D D)

ARCHBISHOP OF ALGOMA, *Metropolitan* (MOST REV G THORNELOE,
　　D.D)
BISHOP OF HURON (RT. REV D. WILLIAMS, D.D).
BISHOP OF ONTARIO (RT REV E J. BIDWELL, D D)
BISHOP OF OTTAWA (RT REV. J. C ROPER, D D).
BISHOP OF TORONTO (RT REV J. F. SWEENY, D D).

BISHOP OF COLUMBIA (RT. REV C. DE V. SCHOFIELD, D D)
BISHOP OF KOOTENAY (RT. REV. A J. DOULL, D.D)
BISHOP OF NEW WESTMINSTER (RT. REV A U DE PENCIER, D.D.)

ARCHBISHOP OF THE WEST INDIES AND BISHOP OF GUIANA, *Metro-
　　politan* (MOST REV. E A. PARRY, D D)
BISHOP OF ANTIGUA (RT REV. E. HUTSON, D D.).
BISHOP OF BARBADOS (RT REV A P. BERKELEY, D.D.).
BISHOP OF HONDURAS, BRITISH (RT. REV E A DUNN, D D)
BISHOP OF JAMAICA (RT REV. G F C DE CARTERET, D.D.)
BISHOP OF NASSAU (RT REV. R G SHEDDEN, D D)

ARCHBISHOP OF SYDNEY, *Primate and Metropolitan* (MOST REV. J. C
　　WRIGHT, D.D)
BISHOP OF ADELAIDE (RT. REV. A. N. THOMAS, D D.).
BISHOP OF GOULBURN (RT REV. L. B RADFORD, D.D).
BISHOP OF GRAFTON (RT. REV. C. H. DRUITT, D D)
BISHOP OF NEWCASTLE (RT REV R STEPHEN, D D).
BISHOP OF NORTH-WEST AUSTRALIA (RT. REV. G. TROWER, D.D).
BISHOP OF RIVERINA (RT REV. E A. ANDERSON, D D).
BISHOP OF TASMANIA (RT REV. R S HAY, D D)
BISHOP OF WILLOCHRA (RT. REV G WHITE, D.D.)

ARCHBISHOP OF MELBOURNE, *Metropolitan* (MOST REV H. LOWTHER
　　CLARKE, D.D.)
BISHOP OF BALLARAT (RT REV. M. H. MAXWELL-GUMBLETON, D D).
BISHOP OF BENDIGO (RT REV D BAKER, D.D.).
BISHOP OF GIPPSLAND (RT. REV G H. CRANSWICK, D D.).

ARCHBISHOP OF BRISBANE, *Metropolitan* (MOST REV. ST. C. G. A. DONALDSON, D D).
BISHOP OF CARPENTARIA (RT. REV H NEWTON, D D)
BISHOP OF NEW GUINEA (RT REV G. SHARP, D.D.)
BISHOP OF NORTH QUEENSLAND (RT. REV. J O. FEETHAM, D D).
BISHOP OF ROCKHAMPTON (RT REV G D HALFORD, D D).

BISHOP OF BUNBURY (RT. REV. C. WILSON, D D)
BISHOP OF KALGOORLIE (RT REV W E. ELSEY, M A)

BISHOP OF AUCKLAND (RT REV A W. AVERILL, D.D.)
BISHOP OF CHRISTCHURCH (RT REV C JULIUS, D D.).
BISHOP OF WAIAPU (RT. REV. W W. SEDGWICK, D D).

BISHOP OF ACCRA (RT REV. M. S. O'RORKE, D.D.).
BISHOP IN ARGENTINA (RT REV E. F. EVERY, D D)
BISHOP IN CHEKIANG (RT. REV. H. J MOLONY, D D)
BISHOP IN COREA (RT REV. M N TROLLOPE, D.D.)
BISHOP OF THE FALKLAND ISLES (RT. REV. N. S DE JERSEY, D D).
BISHOP IN FUKIEN (RT. REV J HIND, D D)
BISHOP OF GIBRALTAR (RT. REV. H J C KNIGHT, D D).
BISHOP IN JERUSALEM (RT. REV. R MACINNES, D.D.)
BISHOP IN KHARTOUM (RT REV. LL. H. GWYNNE, D.D.)
BISHOP IN KWANGSI AND HUNAN (RT REV W BANISTER, D D)
BISHOP IN KYUSHU (RT. REV A LEA, D D)
BISHOP OF LAGOS (RT. REV F. MELVILLE JONES, D.D.)
 ASSISTANT BISHOP OF LAGOS (RT. REV. I OLUWOLE, D.D).
BISHOP OF MOMBASA (RT REV R S HEYWOOD, M A)
BISHOP OF NEWFOUNDLAND (RT REV W C. WHITE, D D).
BISHOP IN NORTH CHINA (RT REV F L NORRIS, D D.).
BISHOP OF NORTHERN RHODESIA (RT REV. A. J W. MAY, D.D).
BISHOP OF NYASALAND (RT. REV. T C FISHER, D D)
BISHOP OF OSAKA (RT. REV. H. J. FOSS, D D)
BISHOP IN PERSIA (RT REV J H LINTON, D D.).
BISHOP IN POLYNESIA (RT. REV. T. C. TWITCHELL, D D)
 ASSISTANT BISHOP FOR TONGA (RT REV A WILLIS, D D).
BISHOP IN SHANTUNG (RT REV G D ILIFF, D.D.)
BISHOP OF SIERRA LEONE (RT REV J WALMSLEY, D D)
BISHOP OF SINGAPORE (RT. REV. C. J FERGUSON-DAVIE, D D)
BISHOP IN SOUTH TOKYO (RT REV C. H. BOUTFLOWER, D D)
BISHOP OF UGANDA (RT. REV. J. J. WILLIS, D.D.).
BISHOP OF KAMPALA (RT REV H GRESFORD JONES, D D).
BISHOP OF VICTORIA, HONGKONG (RT. REV. C R DUPPUY, M A).
BISHOP IN WESTERN CHINA (RT REV W. W CASSELS, D D).
ASSISTANT BISHOP OF WESTERN EQUATORIAL AFRICA (RT. REV A. W HOWELLS, M A)
BISHOP OF ZANZIBAR (RT REV. F WESTON, D D)

BISHOP OF TENNESSEE, *acting-Presiding Bishop* (RT. REV T F. GAILOR, D D)
BISHOP OF ARIZONA (RT REV J W ATWOOD, D D)
BISHOP OF ASHEVILLE (RT. REV. J. M. HORNER, D.D).

BISHOP OF ATLANTA (RT REV H. J. MIKELL, D.D.)
BISHOP OF BETHLEHEM (RT REV. E. TALBOT, D D)
BISHOP OF CONNECTICUT (RT REV. C B BREWSTER, D D).
BISHOP OF HANKOW (RT REV. L. H ROOTS, D D).
BISHOP OF HARRISBURG (RT REV. J H DARLINGTON, D D)
BISHOP OF KANSAS (RT. REV. J. WISE, D D)
BISHOP OF LONG ISLAND (RT. REV. F. BURGESS, D.D)
BISHOP OF MAINE (RT REV. B. BREWSTER, D D).
BISHOP OF MARYLAND (RT. REV. J G MURRAY, D D)
BISHOP OF MASSACHUSETTS (RT REV W LAWRENCE, D.D.)
BISHOP OF MICHIGAN (RT. REV. C D WILLIAMS, D D).
BISHOP OF MILWAUKEE (RT. REV W. W. WEBB, D D)
BISHOP COADJUTOR OF MISSOURI (RT REV. F. F. JOHNSON, D.D.)
BISHOP OF NEBRASKA (RT. REV. E V SHAYLER, D.D.).
BISHOP OF NEWARK (RT. REV. E. S. LINES, D.D.)
   BISHOP COADJUTOR OF NEWARK (RT REV W. R. STEARLY, D.D.).
BISHOP OF NEW JERSEY (RT. REV. P. MATTHEWS, D.D.)
BISHOP OF NEW MEXICO (RT. REV. F B HOWDEN, D.D.)
BISHOP OF NEW YORK (RT. REV. C. S. BURCH, D.D.).
BISHOP OF NORTH CAROLINA (RT. REV. J B CHESHIRE, D.D.).
BISHOP OF NORTH TEXAS (RT REV E A. TEMPLE, D.D.).
BISHOP OF OHIO (RT. REV. W. A LEONARD, D.D.)
   BISHOP COADJUTOR OF OHIO (RT. REV. F. DU MOULIN, D.D.).
BISHOP OF OKLAHOMA (RT. REV T P. THURSTON, D D).
BISHOP OF OLYMPIA (RT REV. F. W KEATOR, D D)
BISHOP OF PENNSYLVANIA (RT. REV. P. M RHINELANDER, D D).
   BISHOP SUFFRAGAN OF PENNSYLVANIA (RT REV T. J GARLAND, D.D.).
BISHOP OF RHODE ISLAND (RT REV. J D PERRY, D D)
BISHOP OF SACRAMENTO (RT REV. W H MORELAND, D D.)
BISHOP OF SOUTHERN BRAZIL (RT REV L L KINSOLVING, D D)
BISHOP OF SOUTH CAROLINA (RT. REV. W. A. GUERRY, D.D.).
BISHOP OF SOUTH DAKOTA (RT. REV H L. BURLESON, D D)
   BISHOP SUFFRAGAN OF SOUTH DAKOTA (RT REV W. P REMINGTON, D.D.)
BISHOP OF SOUTHERN FLORIDA (RT. REV. C. MANN, D D).
BISHOP OF SOUTHERN OHIO (RT. REV. BOYD VINCENT, D.D.)
BISHOP OF TEXAS (RT. REV. G. H. KINSOLVING, D D)
BISHOP OF TOKYO (RT REV J McKIM, D.D)
BISHOP OF VERMONT (RT REV A C A. HALL, D.D.).
BISHOP OF VIRGINIA (RT REV W C BROWN, D D)
BISHOP OF WASHINGTON (RT. REV. A. HARDING, D D)
BISHOP OF WESTERN MASSACHUSETTS (RT. REV. T. F. DAVIES, D D).
BISHOP OF WESTERN MICHIGAN (RT. REV. J. N. McCORMICK, D D.)
BISHOP OF WEST MISSOURI (RT. REV. S C. PARTRIDGE, D D.).
BISHOP OF WESTERN NEBRASKA (RT. REV G A BEECHER, D D)
BISHOP OF WESTERN NEW YORK (RT REV C H. BRENT, D D).
BISHOP OF WEST VIRGINIA (RT. REV. W. L. GRAVATT, D.D.).
BISHOP OF WYOMING (RT. REV N S. THOMAS, D D)
RT REV. E. W. OSBORNE, D.D
RT REV G. MOTT WILLIAMS, D D

[NOTE.—*If it is desired to read this Encyclical Letter in the public services of the Church, it may be found convenient to divide it into two portions. For this purpose, the break should be made at page 17, after the words "* love to men.*"]*

LETTER

To the Faithful in Christ Jesus

We, Archbishops and Bishops of the Holy Catholic Church in full communion with the Church of England, two hundred and fifty-two in number, assembled from divers parts of the earth at Lambeth, under the presidency of the Archbishop of Canterbury, in the year of our Lord 1920, within two years of the ending of the Great War, give you greeting in the name of our Lord and Saviour, Jesus Christ.

We who speak are bearers of the sacred commission of the Ministry given by our Lord through His Apostles to the Church. In His Name we desire to set forth before you the outcome of the grave deliberations to which, after solemn prayer and Eucharist, we have for five weeks devoted ourselves day by day. We take this opportunity of thanking from our hearts all those, both far and near, who have prayed God to give us His Spirit's present aid. We hope that the results of our work may bring encouragement and help to this great circle of intercessors, even in remote parts of the earth. Our deliberations were preceded by careful inquiry upon many sides into the matters about which we speak. In this Letter we propose to give a connected view of these matters, in the hope that it will make our Resolutions more intelligible, and lead some to study them, together with the Reports of our Committees on which they are based.

We find that one idea runs through all our work in this Conference, binding it together into a true unity. It is an idea prevalent and potent throughout the world to-day. It is the idea of Fellowship.

The minds and the hearts of men already go out to this idea. Men never prized the universal fellowship of mankind as they did when the Great War had for the time destroyed it. For four terrible years the loss of international fellowship emphasized its value. But the war which broke one fellowship created others. Nations became associated in alliances, which they cemented with their blood. In every national army, comradeship, novel and intense, united men of different classes and most various traditions. Thousands gained quite a new impression of what human nature might be, when they experienced the fellowship of man with man in danger and death.

9

Comradeship ennobled war. To-day men are asking, Can it not ennoble peace ?

But the power of fellowship was prominent even before the war. Through trade-unions and other societies it had changed the face of industrial life. It bound together workers in science, education, and social reform. It gave its character to our recreations. In these and many other phenomena of the times, there is the same motive taking different forms, the desire for fuller and freer life, and there is the same conviction that it is to be gained by effort in fellowship.

To a world that craves for fellowship we present our message. The secret of life is fellowship. So men feel, and it is true. But fellowship with God is the indispensable condition of human fellowship. The secret of life is the double fellowship, fellowship with God and with men.

This cardinal truth was emphasized by our Lord in words which can never grow old, when He said : " Thou shalt love the Lord thy God with all thy heart and with all thy soul and with all thy mind. This is the great and first commandment." It can never yield the primacy to the second, which is like unto it : " Thou shalt love thy neighbour as thyself." For that primacy belongs to the order of creation. God made man in His own image, and God is love.

Men to-day are tempted to despair of the world and to blame its design. But this at least we can say : the life of men upon earth was designed to give opportunities for love and nothing has defeated that design. Those things which most perplex us, suffering and sin, have been the occasion of the most conspicuous triumphs of love. This design is the clue to the labyrinth of life. We lose our way in the maze whenever we let go this clue.

Men lost the clue and they are always losing it, for they will not keep God in their knowledge, nor love in their hearts. It is ours to recall men to God and to His revealed purposes and His acts which reveal them. It is ours to bid them pause in the hurry and stress of life, in the midst of its trivialities and its tragedy, and contemplate anew the ways of God. He made men for love, that they might love Him and love one another. They rejected His purpose, but He did not abandon it. He chose a nation, and made it in a special sense His own, that within it love of God and men might be cultivated, and that thus it might enlighten the world. Into that nation He sent forth His Son, both to reconcile the world to Himself and to reconcile men one to another. And His Son formed a new and greater Israel, which we call the Church, to carry on His own mission of reconciling men to God and men to men. The foundation and ground of all fellowship is the undeflected will of God, renewing again and again its patient effort to possess, without

destroying, the wills of men And so He has called into being a
fellowship of men, His Church, and sent His Holy Spirit to abide
therein, that by the prevailing attraction of that one Spirit, He,
the one God and Father of all, may win over the whole human
family to that fellowship in Himself, by which alone it can attain
to the fulness of life

This then is the object of the Church In the prosecution
of this object it must take account of every fellowship that
exists among men, must seek to deepen and purify it, and, above
all, to attach it to God. But in order to accomplish its object,
the Church must itself be a pattern of fellowship It is only by
shewing the value and power of fellowship in itself that it can
win the world to fellowship The weakness of the Church in the
world of to-day is not surprising when we consider how the bands
of its own fellowship are loosened and broken.

The truth of this had been slowly working into the consciousness of Christians before the war But the war and its
horrors, waged as it was between so-called Christian
Reunion of nations, drove home the truth with the shock of a
Christen- sudden awakening. Men in all Communions began to
dom. think of the reunion of Christendom, not as a
laudable ambition or a beautiful dream, but as an
imperative necessity Proposals and counter-proposals were
made, some old, some new. Mutual recognition, organic union,
federation, absorption, submission—these phrases indicate the
variety of the programmes put forward Some definite proposals
came from the Mission Field, where the urgency of the work of
evangelization and the birth of national Churches alike demand
a new fellowship Again, in the shadow of suffering and in the
light of sympathy, the ancient Churches of the East drew nearer
to our own than ever before. An official delegation from the
Oecumenical Patriarchate came to London, at the time of our
Conference, to confer with our Committee on the points which
still need mutual explanation between our two Churches The
preparations for the World Conference on Faith and Order had
not only drawn attention in all parts of the world to Christian
unity, but had led to discussions in many quarters which brought
to light unsuspected agreement between the leaders of different
Communions. The great wind was blowing over the whole earth.

Such were the conditions of the time at which our Conference
met. All realized that the subject of reunion was our most
important subject The Bishops brought with them, into the
Conference, very various preconceptions. Different traditions,
different estimates of history, different experiences in the present,
different opinions on current proposals, seemed almost to preclude
the hope of reaching any common mind. The subject of Reunion
was entrusted to the largest Committee ever appointed in a

Lambeth Conference. As their work proceeded, the members of it felt that they were being drawn by a Power greater than themselves to a general agreement. Their conclusions were accepted by the Conference under the same sense of a compelling influence. The decision of the Conference was reached with a unanimity all but complete. It is embodied in our Appeal to all Christian people.

In this Appeal we urge them to try a new approach to reunion ; to adopt a new point of view ; to look up to the reality as it is in God. The unity which we seek exists. It is in God, Who is the perfection of unity, the one Father, the one Lord, the one Spirit, Who gives life to the one Body. Again, the one Body exists. It needs not to be made, nor to be remade, but to become organic and visible. Once more, the fellowship of the members of the one Body exists. It is the work of God, not of man. We have only to discover it, and to set free its activities.

Thus our appeal is in idea and in method a new appeal. If it be prospered, it will change the spirit and direction of our efforts. Terms of reunion must no longer be judged by the success with which they meet the claims and preserve the positions of two or more uniting Communions, but by their correspondence to the common ideal of the Church as God would have it to be. Again, in the past, negotiations for reunion have often started with the attempt to define the measure of uniformity which is essential. The impression has been given that nothing else matters. Now we see that those elements of truth about which differences have arisen are essential to the fulness of the witness of the whole Church. We have no need to belittle what is distinctive in our own interpretation of Christian life : we believe that it is something precious which we hold in trust for the common good. We desire that others should share in our heritage and our blessings, as we wish to share in theirs. It is not by reducing the different groups of Christians to uniformity, but by rightly using their diversity, that the Church can become all things to all men. So long as there is vital connexion with the Head, there is positive value in the differentiation of the members. But we are convinced that this ideal cannot be fulfilled if these groups are content to remain in separation from one another or to be joined together only in some vague federation. Their value for the fulness of Christian life, truth, and witness can only be realised if they are united in the fellowship of one visible society whose members are bound together by the ties of a common faith, common sacraments, and a common ministry. It is towards this ideal of a united and truly Catholic Church that we must all set our minds.

This truer conception of the Church and of the Divine purpose disclosed in its history must regulate our aspirations as well as our endeavours. We cannot suppose, indeed, that we have found a way to solve all difficulties in a moment. The vision must become clear to the general body of Christian men and women, and this will take time. We must all direct our gaze towards it. We must help one another to see what steps lead towards its fulfilment, and what steps lead the other way. The vision points the road to reunion. That road may not be short, but, we believe, it will be sure.

The more our minds are filled with the hopes of seeing the universal fellowship in full and free activity, the more zealous ought we to be to improve and strengthen in every way the fellowship of our own Church. This is one of the most direct and obvious methods of preparing for reunion.

The Anglican Communion.

In our Resolutions we call upon each Church of our Communion to develop its constitutional self-government and to give more and better opportunities for service to all its members. The wider and deeper, the more complete and the more effective is the life of any one Church, the more points of contact will it find with others. We would also communicate to the Churches of our Communion an impression which has forced itself upon us on many occasions in our discussions. Because our Church has spread over the world, and still more because we desire to enter into the world-wide fellowship of a reunited universal Church, we must begin now to clear ourselves of local, sectional, and temporary prepossessions, and cultivate a sense of what is universal and genuinely Catholic, in truth and in life. Our Conferences give us the opportunity of comparing the experience which we have gained in matters of organization, and of bringing together and recording the results for the information of the whole Communion. In this connexion we may mention that at the present meeting we adopted a series of somewhat technical resolutions dealing with the formation of new Provinces and the constitution of the Central Consultative Body. The subject of the Provinces, though important, we will pass over here. The Central Consultative Body acts, in a certain limited way, for the Lambeth Conference in the intervals between its meetings. It is thus one of the links which bind together our fellowship. The characteristics of that fellowship are well worth attention when the reunion of the world-wide Church is in men's thoughts. The fact that the Anglican Communion has become world-wide forces upon it some of the problems which must always beset the unity of the Catholic Church itself. Perhaps, as we ourselves are dealing with these problems, the way will appear in which the future reunited Church must deal with them.

For half a century the Lambeth Conference has more and more served to focus the experience and counsels of our Communion.

But it does not claim to exercise any powers of control or command. It stands for the far more spiritual and more Christian principle of loyalty to the fellowship. The Churches represented in it are indeed independent, but independent with the Christian freedom which recognizes the restraints of truth and of love. They are not free to deny the truth. They are not free to ignore the fellowship. And the objects of our Conferences are to attain an ever deeper apprehension of the truth, and to guard the fellowship with ever increasing appreciation of its value. If the Conference is to attain such objects, it must be because it is itself a fellowship in the Spirit.

The duty of preserving and strengthening the fellowship of the Church belongs specially to a smaller fellowship within it, the fellowship of the ordained ministry. The three Orders of Bishops, Priests, and Deacons have always **The Ministry of Women.** been assisted in their ministry by many others who at different times and in different places have had different names and positions. In a wider and more general sense these all belong to the ministry of the Church; for the special kinds of service which they have to do distinguish them from the main body of Christians, who are commanded in general terms " by love to serve one another." Thus the great fellowship is throughout cemented by service, which is love in action.

There has been much discussion of late about the admission of women to share in the ministry of the Church, both in the wider and in the narrower sense of those words; and the Church must frankly acknowledge that it has under-valued and neglected the gifts of women and has too thanklessly used their work. We have thought well to give in a series of Resolutions what we think to be the general mind of our branch of the Catholic Church at this time about this subject. We feel bound to respect the customs of the Church, not as an iron law, but as results and records of the Spirit's guidance. In such customs there is much which obviously was dictated by reasonable regard to contemporary social conventions. As these differ from age to age and country to country, the use which the Church makes of the service of women will also differ. But this use will be further determined by a more important consideration. It is the peculiar gifts and the special excellences of women which the Church will most wish to use. Its wisdom will be shewn, not in disregarding, but in taking advantage of, the differences between women and men. These considerations seem to have guided the primitive Church to create the Order of Deaconesses. We have recorded our approval of the revival of that Order, and we have attempted to indicate the duties and functions which in our judgement belong to it. We also recognize that God has granted to some women special gifts of spiritual insight and powers of prophetic teaching. We have tried to shew how these gifts can be exercised to the greatest benefit of the Church. The arrangements which we have suggested are not applicable to all countries alike. Yet everywhere the attempt must be made to make room for the Spirit to work, according to the wisdom which He will give, so that the fellowship of the Ministry may be strengthened by the co-operation of women and the fellowship of the Church be enriched by their spiritual gifts.

There is much that the fellowship of the Church lacks for its completeness of life. As a fellowship with God and in God, it has infinite resources of power on which to draw. **Some Movements Outside the Church.** But the tendency to say " the old is good " is particularly strong in the Church. Religious people are apt to feel the goodness of the old so much that they are slow to prove whether there are yet powers of God on which they have never drawn. They are almost equally slow to believe that they might themselves receive the blessings which were given to faith in its primitive freshness. As a result of this, sometimes men and women form fellowships that they may do outside the Church what they ought to have had opportunity to do, and to do better, within it.

One of our committees has dealt with the Christian Faith in relation to Spiritualism, Christian Science, and Theosophy. We commend its Report to all who are interested in these movements. In it the teachings which are connected with them are tested in the light of Christian truth. Tried by the doctrines of the Incarnation and the Cross, they are clearly shewn to involve serious error. It is also shewn that adherents of these movements are drawn into practices and cults which injure their spiritual life, and endanger their loyalty to Christ and to the fellowship of His Church. On the other hand, it must not be forgotten that these movements are very largely symptoms and results of reaction against materialistic views of life. We cannot but sympathize with persons who seek a refuge from the pressure of materialism. It is the part of the Church to afford such a refuge, and, if it fails to do so, there is something wrong with its own life.

There is much in Christian Science which ought to be found within the Church, where it would be supplemented by truths which in Christian Science are neglected. For instance, Church people receive, and must always receive, with all thankfulness, as from God, the help which medical skill and devotion can give. But on the other hand they ought to take more account of the recent growth of knowledge about the power of spirit and mind over body. More than this, they ought to display an intenser faith in their Lord Himself as the source of all healing, bodily and spiritual, and to have bolder expectations of His willingness to respond to their prayers with gracious revelations of His power. They ought to offer far more numerous examples of that repose upon God which is the health of the soul, and secures, in ways which pass understanding, the health of the body. For all these things are the rightful heritage of those who abide in the Divine fellowship.

Religion has promises which we have not fully claimed, not only of the life which now is, but also of the life which is to come. Our fellowship with one another, not less than our fellowship with God, triumphs over death We who belong to the Church's lesser fellowship in this world are not separated from, but are one with, those who belong to the Church's higher fellowship in the other world This is, in part, what we mean by the Communion or Fellowship of Saints The distance between our temporary and our permanent home, between earth and heaven, is not great. Christ and His Apostles made this clear, and the Christian experience of centuries has confirmed it. Belief in this reality and the nearness of the other world has been deepened by the war. The bereaved heart of mankind with earnest, if not always wise, endeavour is straining to bridge the space that lies between It is in this endeavour that many distracted souls turn to spiritualism for help, not realizing that the Church has abundant treasures of comfort, and assurance of the world beyond this, with which to bring to the sorrowing the solace which is the right and the heritage of Christians It is for the commissioned teachers of the Church so to present the Communion of Saints as to make it a satisfying force in the life of mourners. Whatever new triumphs of faith remain to be achieved and whatever new voices of comfort are waiting for utterance, the bond of love, rightly understood, will continue to be strong enough to carry the bereaved through the days of mourning and the discipline of separation till the day breaks and the shadows flee. Here, as in all fellowship, there are silences and limitations which cannot be wholly done away while earth lasts. But through them and beyond them fellowship abides.

Fellowship in this life, whether with God or with one another, is but the preliminary stage in an eternal progress While the spiritualist seeks light upon the future life through communication with the departed, the theosophist seeks the clue to his own destiny in the mysteries of his own being Here again the Christian faith gives us all that we need for life and work. That faith bids us look onward from glory to glory, in the ever closer union of the spirit of man with the Christ who is God and was made man, and not merely in the evolution of a Christ within, who is but the higher self of man. Here again fellowship is the path and the goal. The hidden man of the heart, who is now being fashioned by the one Spirit after the likeness of the one Christ, is no lonely seeker after truth, no disciple of an esoteric brotherhood, but a citizen of a spiritual kingdom in which all sorts and conditions of men in every race and nation are being trained to feel the power of God and to fulfil the purpose of God for the whole world.

We have spoken of the Church and of those things which it lacks. If it is to be a perfect fellowship, as it ought to be, it must recover them, especially unity and power. We would end this section of our Letter by pleading earnestly with Church people to use the only means by which the Church can regain those great gifts. The first is prayer. Pray without ceasing, without wavering, faithfully, instantly, fervently. Prayer is the source of all our strength. The second is to obey the Lord's command, and more earnestly and more devoutly to partake of the Sacrament of His Body and Blood. In it offer yourselves with your souls and bodies, to be a reasonable, holy, and lively sacrifice in union with His Sacrifice. In it learn from Him the way of fellowship, with God and with man, and receive in Him the power to share His love to His Father and His love to men.

From the fellowship of the Church, what it ought to be and what it ought to contain, we now pass to other fellowships which **Marriage** exist among men by the will of God. For these fellow-**and the** ships too there is only one inspiration, and that is the **Family.** Spirit of God. The Church, in which it has pleased God to dwell by His Spirit, ought therefore to have a message for all these fellowships.

The fellowship between man and woman in marriage was the earliest which God gave to the human race. "From the beginning of the creation," as our Lord reminded us, God made them male and female. What our Lord adds about marriage is not given as new legislation, but as a declaration of God's original purpose. The man and his wife are no longer twain, but one flesh : and those whom God has joined together, man is not to put asunder. This revelation about God's purpose gives the keynote to all that the Church has to teach about marriage. Because it can found its teaching upon the will and act of God in making the union, the Church can go on to teach how God will complete it. He will work, as those who wait for Him well know, the miracle by which the two lives become one, yet so that each life becomes greater and better than it could have been alone. But marriage is not ordained only to give opportunity for the development of those two lives in unity. It has essentially the aim of bringing other lives into the world. Its indissolubility should secure to the children the continued care and love of both their parents, so long as they live. The State's obvious interest in the children should lead it to preserve

c

the strictness of marriage law. On the other hand it is the
purpose of God for themselves and for their children that
Christian parents should regard. On the fellowship begun in
their union and widened into the fellowship of their home, they
will build up their nation according to the purpose of God ;
and not only the nation but also the Church ; for He, after
Whom the carpenter's household will ever be called the Holy
Family, wills to build every generation of His Church on holy
families.

We cannot forget how He Who was the centre of the Holy
Family became afterwards the succourer and saviour of some
of those who had strayed furthest away from the sanctities of
home. He raises up in His Church from age to age compassionate
spirits, who by His aid follow the example of His winning compassion. Our Committee has touched upon this part of the
Church's work, and urged the great need that is now felt for more
helpers in it. We note with interest how the spirit of fellowship
is stirring here also, and how it is now agreed that the love and
brightness of comradeship should surround those unhappy ones
as they retrace their steps to a truer life.

The relation of men one to another in industry or trade is
another fellowship which God intended to exist and created
to be good. Yet to-day we are confronted with a
Industry world-wide upheaval and embittered antagonism in
and social relations, the course of which none can foresee.
Commerce. We seem to be involved in an internecine conflict
between capital and labour in which each aims
at an exclusive supremacy. Any such supremacy would be
inconsistent with the Christian ideal of fellowship. And the
Church insists that, in its essential nature, industry is not a
conflict, but a fellowship. Again, every trade or profession
ought to be producing something which men want and ought
to want, and so far each is doing service to the community.
But in industrial life all such service depends on combined
effort. It is rendered in co-operation. The message of
Christianity in this matter is to make men see that here they
can and must " in love serve one another." To all concerned,
employer and employed, director and workman, investor of
money and investor of brain or muscle—to all alike the Church
must say : " Put first your service to the community and your
fellowship in that service. Do your work heartily, keenly,
carefully as to God, because you are benefiting His children.
Have good will, and expect others to have it. Rearrange your
mutual relations, as men co-operating in fellowship, not competing
in suspicion and hostility." These are fundamental principles.
Beyond them lies the whole region of practical application.
In the technical side of economics, which is a science for experts,

the Church has no authority. But whenever in the working out of economic or of political theory moral issues are directly involved, the Church has a duty to see that the requirements of righteousness are faced and fairly met. The Church will, for instance, maintain that fellowship is endangered if all who serve do not share equitably in the results of labour. For this is part of Christian justice. The Church will fearlessly claim that the human character of every worker is more sacred than his work ; that his worth as a child of God and member of the fellowship must not be forgotten, or imperilled by any form of industrial slavery. For this belongs to the spirit of Christian liberty. In all such things the Church will, under the guidance of the Holy Spirit, proclaim its message of brotherhood and mutual service, founded on the Divine purpose for men, and will aid the community in giving active expression to it. But our hope throughout is in the Spirit of God. In no other way, as we believe, can society recover itself than by recovering the plan of God for its well-being, and by reliance on His inspiration for realizing that plan. Such are the principles and thoughts which underlie our Resolutions on Industrial and Social Problems.

We pass on to the relation between nations. We cannot believe that the effect of the coming of the Kingdom of God upon earth will be to abolish nations. Holy Scripture **Inter-** emphasizes the value of national life and indicates **national** its permanence. The sense of nationality seems to **Relations.** be a natural instinct. The love which Christ pours into the hearts that are His, makes men cease to hate each other because they belong to different nations. Within redeemed humanity nations will not cease to exist, but nationality itself will be redeemed. We need not despair of this consummation because of any wrongs which have been done in the name of nationality, however recent and however appalling.

Thus the purpose of God for the nations, as we conceive it, is that they should form a fellowship, as of a brotherhood or a family. They are intended, as nations, by love to serve one another. They are intended to develop distinctive gifts and characters, and to contribute them to the common good. There is no place in this ideal for jealousy or hatred, for ruthless competition, and for the ambition to conquer and to enslave. Nor does the imposition of peace upon the world by fear of the strong arm bring this ideal much nearer. For this ideal is essentially an ideal of freedom, the freedom of brothers in a family, wherein the immature and the weak have carefully secured to them the chance to grow and to grow strong.

We commend to all Christian people the principles which underlie the League of Nations, the most promising and the most systematic attempt to advance towards the ideal of the family

of nations which has ever been projected.   It has deeply stirred
the hopes of those who long for peace on earth and increase of
fellowship.   But if any such League is to have success it will
need the enthusiastic and intelligent support of millions of men
and women.   It is not enough that Governments should agree
to it, or statesmen work for it.   The hearts and minds of the
people in all countries must be behind it.   In all nations a
great change is needed, and is needed now.   War-weariness cannot unite and is not uniting us.   Neither the sufferings of some
countries nor the ambitions of others are making much impression
on a paralysed world.   The world needs to recover feeling, but
the feeling must be right and true.   Before either peace or freedom can be established in security and joy, the fires of brother-
love must leap up in the hearts of the nations.   This great change
requires a miracle, but it is a change that can be wrought by the
one Spirit of fellowship, which is the Spirit of God.   We must
subject our wills and open our hearts to His influence, that
He may work that miracle in the world.

It will be naturally and rightly said that the great ideal of
the brotherhood of nations involves for its full realization the
thorough permeation of the nations with Christ's
Spirit.   The conversion of the nations is the only
Missionary real hope for the world.
Problems.
It is a curious coincidence that all the most
prominent problems in the Mission Field to-day are
in some way connected with nationality.   The Report of our
Committee traverses the whole ground.   We would here indicate
only the salient points.

"These that have turned the world upside down are come
hither also."   Many others besides the men of Thessalonica have
recognized that Christianity is a revolutionary force.   It cannot
be otherwise.   The preaching of the Kingdom of God is always,
as it was at the first, also the preaching of a change of mind.
It is certain to make people see that " the manner of life handed
down from their fathers " is in some, or perhaps many, respects
" vain."   Whether missionaries emphasize this, or leave it to be
inferred, they are sure to incur suspicion and arouse resentment.
But to-day they are coming to see that some of this suspicion
and resentment is due to their own faulty conception of their
object

They have been content to make disciples out of all the
nations   They have not remembered that their Master in fact
commanded them to make all the nations His disciples   In other
words they have not taken due account of the value of nationality.
The aim of missions is not only to make Christians, but to make
Christian nations.   The principle has consequences, both negative
and positive, which are daily becoming clearer.   No community

of Christians has a right to attempt to produce a replica of itself in a foreign country which it evangelizes. Neither forms of worship, nor methods of thought, nor social institutions belonging to one race ought to be imposed on another Nor will evangelism or pastorate for longer than necessary be retained in foreign hands

Foreign missionaries should set before themselves one ideal, and one only: to plant the Catholic Church in every land They must remember that the Catholic Church needs the fulness of the nations They must long to see national life putting on Christ, and national thought interpreting His truth. The more they have valued their own nationality, the more they should respect the nationality of others. They do not go out to obliterate other men's nationality, but to bring it near to Christ Who can exalt and complete it. They do not go out to propagate their national Church, but to add another national Church to the Church Catholic. They carry with them warnings and lessons from the history of national Churches. They will be on their guard against that sectarian spirit which is the danger of national isolation No foreigner can forecast, still less invent, the lines of national development in religion The foreign missionary therefore must give his strength to making known Christ in the fulness of His Person, His work, and His revelation of the Father, together with the great inheritance of Catholic tradition and the glory of the fellowship of the Catholic Church He must leave to the converts the task of finding out their national response to the revelation of God in Christ, and their national way of walking in the fellowship of the Saints by the help of the One Spirit. Thus will the glory of the nations be brought into the Holy City.

But not only does the Church need every nation to be evangelized It needs also the help of every nation in evangelization. It has been a consequence of the late war that missionaries of certain nations are forbidden to work in the greater part of the world. As Christians, we cannot acquiesce in this prohibition, except as a temporary measure. The command of Christ is obligatory on those nations, as on our own. Nor can the missionary cause afford to lose their assistance But if this claim, which we thus advance in the Name of Christ, is to command the attention of statesmen, the standard of missionary single-mindedness must be kept very high No one can be a politician as well as a missionary, without endangering the credit of Christian Missions as a whole If missions are not to be at the mercy of measures of political expediency, missionaries must be plainly seen to have no object or motive, no thought beyond the spreading of the Kingdom of God.

We have devoted so much space to the relation of nations and the national spirit to missions, because that is the out-

standing problem of the Mission Field to-day.   But we would not
be misunderstood.   Each of us belongs by his birth to some
one of the many nations of the world.   But every Christian
belongs by his second birth to one holy nation, which is God's
own possession.   When loyalty to his own nation comes into
conflict with loyalty to that holy nation of which Christ is King,
a Christian can have no doubt which loyalty must give way
" He that loveth father and mother more than me," said Jesus
Christ, " is not worthy of me."   National loyalty has often led
men into exclusiveness, jealousy and hatred, which are far
from Christ's purpose   No selfishness in the world has been
so persistent or so ruthless as national selfishness.   It is to save
men from such wickedness that Jesus Christ binds them together
into one holy nation   In the fellowship of this great unity
nationality finds its redemption · while national characteristics
are preserved for noble use and mutual benefit.   But the love of
God encompasses all and reconciles both men and nations in
the brotherhood of redeemed humanity.

To a world full of trouble and perplexity, of fear and despair,
of disconnected effort and aimless exertion, we present what
we have been permitted to see of the purpose of God
Conclusion. It is enough to guide us.   But, if it often seems that
the message of religion is too general and its application
to details too difficult, then it is our duty to recall to ourselves
that we have to do, not with a theory, but with a Person.   God
is working His purpose out.   If in simplicity we give ourselves
to Him, He will work with us beyond our understanding : and
we shall have contributed to the fellowship of man, because we
have been working in fellowship with God

Signed on behalf of the Conference,

RANDALL CANTUAR :

THEODORE PETRIBURG.   ⎫
H. H. MONTGOMERY (Bishop) ⎬ *Secretaries*
                                             ⎭
G. K. A BELL, *Assistant Secretary*

August 7th, 1920.

NOTE.

It may be well to make clear the manner of our deliberations.
The subjects proposed for consideration were first brought before us in
Sessions of the whole Conference, lasting for six full days, from Monday,
July 5th to Saturday, July 10th   Having been there set forth in outline,

they were then referred to large and carefully chosen Committees, and the Reports of these Committees, with the Resolutions which they had prepared, were subsequently laid before the Conference, meeting again to consider them in full session from Monday, July 26th, to Saturday, August 7th By this procedure we have been able to secure both the detailed study which is the especial task of a Committee (a study greatly aided by the essays, Reports and papers which had been prepared for us), and that weight of judgement which belongs to the decisions of an assembly gathered from all parts of the world and bringing to the process of deliberation the manifold experience and knowledge acquired under widely different conditions in widely sundered fields of labour.

The judgement of the Conference is expressed in the Resolutions, eighty in number, appended to this Letter   These, and these alone, are affirmed by the Conference The Reports, which are also printed herewith, have been received by the Conference, and the Conference has directed that they should be published; but the responsibility for the statements and opinions which they contain rests with the several Committees by whom they were prepared.

RESOLUTIONS FORMALLY ADOPTED BY THE CONFERENCE OF 1920.

CHRISTIANITY AND INTERNATIONAL RELATIONS.

1. We rejoice that in these times of peril God is giving to His Church a fresh vision of His purpose to establish a Kingdom in which all the nations of the earth shall be united as one family in righteousness and peace. We hold that this can only come through the acceptance of the sovereignty of our Lord Jesus Christ and of His teaching, and through the application of the principles of brotherhood, justice, and unselfishness, to individuals and nations alike.

2. The Conference calls upon the citizens of all nations to promote in every way the resumption of the efforts, interrupted by the War, to increase international comity and goodwill, and to secure expression for these by an increased recognition of international law and custom.

3. The Conference, heartily endorsing the views of its Committee as to the essentially Christian basis of the League of Nations, is of opinion that steps should immediately be taken, whether by co-operation or concurrent action, whereby the whole Church of Christ may be enabled with one voice to urge the principles of the League of Nations upon the peoples of the world.

4. We hold that the peace of the world, no less than Christian principle, demands the admission of Germany and other nations into the League of Nations at the earliest moment which the conditions render possible.

5. The Conference commends the Report of its Committee on International Relations to the careful consideration of the Churches of the Anglican Communion, both in their Assemblies and in other ways, and urges upon all Church members the importance of supporting the League of Nations Union.

6. It is the duty of all supporters of the League of Nations to set their face against injustice to the indigenous or native races, and particularly in regard to such matters as the tenure of land, forced labour, and the trade in intoxicating liquors, and also the morphia traffic in China, and other abuses.

7. The Conference records its protest against the colour-prejudice among the different races of the world, which not only hinders intercourse, but gravely imperils the peace of the future.

8. The Conference, believing that nations no less than individuals are members one of another, expresses its grave concern at the evidence as to the disease and distress from which the populations in large tracts of Europe and Asia are suffering. It therefore calls upon all Christian men and women to support by every means in their power the action which is being taken, both by Governments and by voluntary associations, for the relief of this suffering.

REUNION OF CHRISTENDOM.

9. The Conference adopts and sends forth the following Appeal to all Christian people :

AN APPEAL TO ALL CHRISTIAN PEOPLE

FROM THE BISHOPS ASSEMBLED IN THE LAMBETH CONFERENCE OF 1920.

WE, Archbishops, Bishops Metropolitan, and other Bishops of the Holy Catholic Church in full communion with the Church of England, in Conference assembled, realizing the responsibility which rests upon us at this time, and sensible of the sympathy and the prayers of many, both within and without our own Communion, make this appeal to all Christian people.

We acknowledge all those who believe in our Lord Jesus Christ, and have been baptized into the name of the Holy Trinity, as sharing with us membership in the universal Church of Christ which is His Body. We believe that the Holy Spirit has called us in a very solemn and special manner to associate ourselves in penitence and prayer with all those who deplore the divisions of Christian people, and are inspired by the vision and hope of a visible unity of the whole Church.

I. We believe that God wills fellowship. By God's own act this fellowship was made in and through Jesus Christ, and its life is in His Spirit. We believe that it is God's purpose to manifest this fellowship, so far as this world is concerned, in an outward, visible, and united society, holding one faith, having its own recognized officers, using God-given means of grace, and inspiring all its members to the world-wide service of the Kingdom of God. This is what we mean by the Catholic Church.

II. This united fellowship is not visible in the world to-day. On the one hand there are other ancient episcopal Communions in East and West, to whom ours is bound by many ties of common faith and tradition. On the other hand there are the great non-episcopal Communions, standing for rich elements of truth, liberty and life which might otherwise have been obscured or neglected. With them we are closely linked by many affinities, racial, historical and spiritual. We cherish the earnest hope that all these Communions, and our own, may be led by the Spirit into the unity of the Faith and of the knowledge of the Son of God. But in fact we are all organized in different groups, each one keeping to itself gifts that rightly belong to the whole fellowship, and tending to live its own life apart from the rest.

III. The causes of division lie deep in the past, and are by no means simple or wholly blameworthy. Yet none can doubt that self-will, ambition, and lack of charity among Christians have been principal factors in the mingled process, and that these, together with blindness to the sin of disunion, are still mainly responsible for the breaches of Christendom. We acknowledge this condition of broken fellowship to be contrary to God's will, and we desire frankly to confess our share in the guilt of thus crippling the Body of Christ and hindering the activity of His Spirit.

IV. The times call us to a new outlook and new measures. The Faith cannot be adequately apprehended and the battle of the Kingdom cannot be worthily fought while the body is divided, and is thus unable to grow up into the fulness of the life of Christ. The time has come, we believe, for all the separated groups of Christians to agree in forgetting the things which are behind and reaching out towards the goal of a reunited Catholic Church. The removal of the barriers which have arisen between them will only be brought about by a new comradeship of those whose faces are definitely set this way.

The vision which rises before us is that of a Church, genuinely Catholic, loyal to all Truth, and gathering into its fellowship all "who profess and call themselves Christians," within whose visible unity all the treasures of faith and order, bequeathed as a heritage by the past to the present, shall be possessed in common, and made serviceable to the whole Body of Christ. Within this unity Christian Communions now separated from one another would retain much that has long been distinctive in their methods of worship and service. It is through a rich diversity of life and devotion that the unity of the whole fellowship will be fulfilled.

V. This means an adventure of goodwill and still more of faith, for nothing less is required than a new discovery of the creative resources of God. To this adventure we are convinced that God is now calling all the members of His Church

VI. We believe that the visible unity of the Church will be found to involve the whole-hearted acceptance of :—

The Holy Scriptures, as the record of God's revelation of Himself to man, and as being the rule and ultimate standard of faith, and the Creed commonly called Nicene, as the sufficient statement of the Christian faith, and either it or the Apostles' Creed as the Baptismal confession of belief :

The divinely instituted sacraments of Baptism and the Holy Communion, as expressing for all the corporate life of the whole fellowship in and with Christ :

A ministry acknowledged by every part of the Church as possessing not only the inward call of the Spirit, but also the commission of Christ and the authority of the whole body.

VII. May we not reasonably claim that the Episcopate is the one means of providing such a ministry? It is not that we call in question for a moment the spiritual reality of the ministries of those Communions which do not possess the Episcopate. On the contrary we thankfully acknowledge that these ministries have been manifestly blessed and owned by the Holy Spirit as effective means of grace. But we submit that considerations alike of history and of present experience justify the claim which we make on behalf of the Episcopate. Moreover, we would urge that it is now and will prove to be in the future the best instrument for maintaining the unity and continuity of the Church. But we greatly desire that the office of a Bishop should be everywhere exercised in a representative and constitutional manner, and more truly express all that ought to be involved for the life of the Christian Family in the title of Father-in-God Nay more, we eagerly look forward to the day when through its acceptance in a united Church we may all share in that grace which is pledged to the members of the whole body in the apostolic rite of the laying-on of hands, and in the joy and fellowship of a Eucharist in which as one Family we may together, without any doubtfulness of mind, offer to the one Lord our worship and service.

VIII. We believe that for all, the truly equitable approach to union is by the way of mutual deference to one another's consciences. To this end, we who send forth this appeal would say that if the authorities of other Communions should so desire, we are persuaded that, terms of union having been otherwise satisfactorily adjusted, Bishops and clergy of our Communion would willingly accept from these authorities a form of commission or recognition which would commend our ministry to their congregations, as having its place in the one family life. It is not in our power to know how far this suggestion may be acceptable to those to whom we offer it. We can only say that we offer it in all sincerity as a token of our longing that all ministries of grace, theirs and ours, shall be available for the service of our Lord in a united Church.

It is our hope that the same motive would lead ministers who have not received it to accept a commission through episcopal ordination, as obtaining for them a ministry throughout the whole fellowship

In so acting no one of us could possibly be taken to repudiate his past ministry God forbid that any man should repudiate a past experience rich in spiritual blessings for himself and others Nor would any of us be dishonouring the Holy Spirit of God, Whose call led us all to our several ministries, and Whose power enabled us to perform them. We shall be publicly and formally seeking additional recognition of a new call to wider service in a reunited Church, and imploring for ourselves God's grace and strength to fulfil the same

IX. The spiritual leadership of the Catholic Church in days to come, for which the world is manifestly waiting, depends upon the readiness with which each group is prepared to make sacrifices for the sake of a common fellowship, a common ministry, and a common service to the world.

We place this ideal first and foremost before ourselves and our own people We call upon them to make the effort to meet the demands of a new age with a new outlook. To all other Christian people whom our words may reach we make the same appeal We do not ask that any one Communion should consent to be absorbed in another. We do ask that all should unite in a new and great endeavour to recover and to manifest to the world the unity of the Body of Christ for which He prayed.

---

10. The Conference recommends to the authorities of the Churches of the Anglican Communion that they should, in such ways and at such times as they think best, formally invite the authorities of other Churches within their areas to confer with them concerning the possibility of taking definite steps to

co-operate in a common endeavour, on the lines set forth in the
above Appeal, to restore the unity of the Church of Christ.

11. The Conference recognizes that the task of effecting union
with other Christian Communions must be undertaken by the
various national, regional, or provincial authorities of the
Churches within the Anglican Communion, and confidently
commits to them the carrying out of this task on lines that are
in general harmony with the principles underlying its Appeal
and Resolutions

12. The Conference approves the following statements as
representing the counsel which it is prepared to give to the
Bishops, Clergy and other members of our own Communion on
various subjects which bear upon the problems of reunion.

(A) *In view of prospects and projects of reunion—*

(i) A Bishop is justified in giving occasional authorization
to ministers, not episcopally ordained, who in his judgement are
working towards an ideal of union such as is described in our
Appeal, to preach in churches within his Diocese, and to clergy
of the Diocese to preach in the churches of such ministers :

(ii) The Bishops of the Anglican Communion will not question
the action of any Bishop who, in the few years between the
initiation and the completion of a definite scheme of union, shall
countenance the irregularity of admitting to Communion the
baptized but unconfirmed Communicants of the non-episcopal
congregations concerned in the scheme :

(iii) The Conference gives its general approval to the suggestions contained in the report of the Sub-Committee on Reunion
with Non-Episcopal Churches in reference to the status and work
of ministers who may remain after union without episcopal
ordination (see pages 142 and 143.)

(B) *Believing, however, that certain lines of action might
imperil both the attainment of its ideal and the unity of its own
Communion, the Conference declares that—*

(i) It cannot approve of general schemes of intercommunion
or exchange of pulpits :

(ii) In accordance with the principle of Church order set forth
in the Preface to the Ordinal attached to the Book of Common
Prayer, it cannot approve the celebration in Anglican churches
of the Holy Communion for members of the Anglican Church by
ministers who have not been episcopally ordained ; and that it
should be regarded as the general rule of the Church that Anglican
communicants should receive Holy Communion only at the
hands of ministers of their own Church, or of Churches in communion therewith.

(C) In view of doubts and varieties of practice which have caused difficulties in the past, the Conference declares that—

(i) Nothing in these Resolutions is intended to indicate that the rule of Confirmation as conditioning admission to the Holy Communion must necessarily apply to the case of baptized persons who seek Communion under conditions which in the Bishop's judgement justify their admission thereto.

(ii) In cases in which it is impossible for the Bishop's judgement to be obtained beforehand the priest should remember that he has no canonical authority to refuse Communion to any baptized person kneeling before the Lord's Table (unless he be excommunicate by name, or, in the canonical sense of the term, a cause of scandal to the faithful) ; and that, if a question may properly be raised as to the future admission of any such person to Holy Communion, either because he has not been confirmed or for other reasons, the priest should refer the matter to the Bishop for counsel or direction.

13. The Conference recommends that, wherever it has not already been done, Councils representing all Christian Communions should be formed within such areas as may be deemed most convenient, as centres of united effort to promote the physical, moral, and social welfare of the people, and the extension of the rule of Christ among all nations and over every region of human life.

14. It is important to the cause of reunion that every branch of the Anglican Communion should develop the constitutional government of the Church and should make a fuller use of the capacities of its members for service.

15. The Conference urges on every branch of the Anglican Communion that it should prepare its members for taking their part in the universal fellowship of the re-united Church, by setting before them the loyalty which they owe to the universal Church, and the charity and understanding which are required of the members of so inclusive a society.

16. We desire to express our profound thankfulness for the important movements towards unity which, during the last twelve years, have taken place in many parts of the world, and for the earnest desire for reunion which has been manifested both in our own Communion and among the Churches now separated from us. In particular, the Conference has heard with sympathetic and hopeful interest of the preliminary meeting of the proposed

World Conference on Faith and Order about to be held at Geneva, and earnestly prays that its deliberations may tend towards the reunion of the Christian Church.

---

17. We desire to express our deep sympathy with the Church of Russia in the terrible persecution which it has in many places suffered We earnestly trust that in the providence of God its difficulties may speedily be removed, and that it may be enabled in renewed life and strength so to carry on its work unhindered as to further, in the life of the Russian people, whatsoever things are true and just, whatsoever things are lovely and of good report.

18. The Conference heartily thanks the Œcumenical Patriarchate for the mission of the Metropolitan of Demotica and others to confer with its members on questions concerning the relations between the Anglican and Eastern Churches, and expresses its grateful appreciation of the great help given to its Committee by the Delegation

19. The Conference welcomes the appointment by the Archbishop of Canterbury of an " Eastern Churches' Committee " on a permanent basis, in pursuance of Resolution 61 of the Conference of 1908 , and looks forward hopefully to the work of that Committee, in conjunction with similar Committees appointed in Constantinople and Athens, as helping greatly to forward the cause of reunion with the Orthodox Church.

20. The Conference expresses its heartfelt sympathy with the Armenian, Assyrian, and Syrian Jacobite Christians in the persecutions which they have been called upon to endure, deploring with indignation the terrible massacres that have taken place among them both before and during the Great War ; and earnestly prays that in the rearrangement of the political affairs of the East they may be granted a righteous government and freedom from oppression for the future.

21. The Conference has received with satisfaction its Committee's report of the investigations that have been made during the last twelve years with regard to the present doctrinal position of the Separated Churches of the East , and, without expressing an opinion as to the past, believes that these investigations have gone far towards shewing that any errors as to the Incarnation of our Lord, which may at some period of their history have been attributed to them, have at any rate now passed away.

22. The Conference repeats the proposal made by the Conference of 1908 that, when any of the Separated Churches of the East desire closer relations with us, and wish for the establishment of occasional intercommunion, and give satisfactory assurances as to their faith, such relations should at once be established.

23. The Conference respectfully requests the Archbishop of Canterbury to take advantage of any opportunity that may arise to enter into friendly relations with these Churches, and to inform the authorities of the Orthodox Eastern Church of any steps that may be taken in the direction of intercommunion with them. Similar action should be taken with regard to informing the Metropolitans of our own Communion.

24. The Conference welcomes the Report of the Commission appointed after the last Conference entitled, " The Church of England and the Church of Sweden," and, accepting the conclusions there maintained on the succession of the Bishops of the Church of Sweden and the conception of the priesthood set forth in its standards, recommends that members of that Church, qualified to receive the Sacrament in their own Church, should be admitted to Holy Communion in ours. It also recommends that on suitable occasions permission should be given to Swedish ecclesiastics to give addresses in our churches.

If the authorities of any province of the Anglican Communion find local irregularities in the order or practice of the Church of Sweden outside that country, they may legitimately, within their own region, postpone any such action as is recommended in this Resolution until they are satisfied that these irregularities have been removed

25. We recommend further that in the event of an invitation being extended to an Anglican Bishop or Bishops to take part in the consecration of a Swedish Bishop, the invitation should, if possible, be accepted, subject to the approval of the Metropolitan We also recommend that, in the first instance, as an evident token of the restoration of closer relations between the two Churches, if possible more than one of our Bishops should take part in the Consecration.

26. The Conference thanks the Old Catholic Bishops for their explanation, in response to the letter of the Archbishop of Canterbury, of their action in consecrating the Rev. A. H. Mathew to the Episcopate in 1908, and repeats the desire expressed at previous Conferences to maintain and strengthen the friendly relations which exist between the Churches of the Anglican Communion and the ancient Church of Holland and

D

the Old Catholic Churches, especially in Germany, Switzerland and Austria.

27. We regret that on a review of all the facts we are unable to regard the so-called Old Catholic Church in Great Britain (under the late Bishop Mathew and his successors), and its extensions overseas, as a properly constituted Church, or to recognize the orders of its ministers, and we recommend that, in the event of any of its ministers desiring to join our communion, who are in other respects duly qualified, they should be ordained *sub conditione* in accordance with the provisions suggested in the Report of our Committee

28. The Conference recommends that the same course be followed, as occasion may require, in the case of persons claiming to have received consecration or ordination from any "episcopi vagantes," whose claims we are unable to recognize.

29. The Conference, while welcoming the Report of the Committee appointed by the Conference of 1908 on the *Unitas Fratrum* or Moravians, regrets that it is unable to recommend any such action being taken as is suggested in resolutions 70–72 of that Conference so long as the *Unitas* retains its practice of the administration of Confirmation and the celebration of Holy Communion by deacons, but hopes that, in the event of the *Unitas* changing its rules in these matters, negotiations with individual Provinces of the *Unitas* may be resumed, and believes that in this case there would be good prospect of such negotiations being brought to a satisfactory conclusion

30. We recommend with a view to this end that the Archbishop of Canterbury be respectfully requested to reappoint with additional members the Committee appointed at the last Conference ; and we hope that, in the event of all the remaining difficulties being removed to his satisfaction, with the concurrence of the Central Consultative Body of the Lambeth Conference, the action suggested in the Resolutions of the Conference of 1908 may take place without further delay.

31. The Conference regrets that it is unable to recommend the acceptance of the proposals of the " Southern Synod " of the " Reformed Episcopal Church " in England for reunion with the Church of England, and, while unable to advise the acceptance of other proposals for corporate union with the Reformed Episcopal Church, recommends that, if applications for admission into the English Church are made by individual ministers of that Communion, such applications should be sympathetically received, and the ministers, if in all respects equal to the standard and requirements of the Church of England, be ordained *sub conditione*

MISSIONARY PROBLEMS.

32. The Conference declares its conviction that the present critical position of the world calls, as perhaps never before, for the presentation of Jesus Christ and His redemption to every race and individual ; and, in view of the urgent need for workers in many dioceses overseas, earnestly appeals to men, both clerical and lay, and to women, to dedicate themselves to the service of the Church in those dioceses.

33. The normal method of missions is that in which the whole Church, within any area, acts as a missionary body expressly organized for that function, and the principle which underlies this method is capable of universal application While we humbly thank God for the work of the Missionary Societies, we consider that these Societies, where they exist, should not stand outside the one organization, but should be elements in it, co-ordinated, whether by a central advisory council or otherwise, under the supreme Synodical Authority, but retaining severally such degrees of independence as the conditions of their efficiency demand.

34. The Conference thankfully recognizes the practical steps which Missionary Societies and Boards have taken towards the realization of the ultimate aim of all Mission work, namely, the establishment of self-governing, self-supporting, and self-extending Churches, from which outside control has been withdrawn at the earliest moment, so as to allow the free expression of their national character.

It would urge further that the call for such action is in the present day more insistent than ever before, and believes that, generally speaking, the Societies and Boards can best achieve their purpose by making their work centre from the first in the Church rather than in the mission organization, and in particular—

(1) By the establishment of Councils which shall be fully representative of the congregations, and have real responsibilities of government ,

(2) By substituting for committees and councils representative chiefly of the mission and its subscribers, Diocesan Boards and Committees, and in general associating all their work with the Diocesan organization ;

(3) By entrusting to these local bodies a real share in the financial control and general direction of the work of the Mission ;

(4) By giving the widest freedom to indigenous workers to develop the work in their own countries on lines in accordance with their national character.

35. The territorial Episcopate has been the normal development in the Catholic Church, but we recognize that difference of race and language sometimes requires that provision should be made in a Province for freedom of development of races side by side ; the solution in each case must be left with the Province, but we are clear that the ideal of the one Church should never be obscured.

36. While maintaining the authority of the Book of Common Prayer as the Anglican standard of doctrine and practice, we consider that liturgical uniformity should not be regarded as a necessity throughout the Churches of the Anglican Communion. The conditions of the Church in many parts of the Mission Field render inapplicable the retention of that Book as the one fixed liturgical model.

37. Although the inherent right of a Diocesan Bishop to put forth or sanction liturgical forms is subject to such limitations as may be imposed by higher synodical authority, it is desirable that such authority should not be too rigidly exercised so long as those features are retained which are essential to the safeguarding of the unity of the Anglican Communion.

38. The Conference recommends the appointment of a Committee of students of liturgical questions which would be ready to advise any Diocese or Province on the Form and Matter of services proposed for adoption, and requests the Archbishop of Canterbury to take such steps as he deems best to give early effect to this Resolution.

39. It is of very real importance that the Marriage Law of the Church should be understood and administered as far as possible consistently, in all parts of the Anglican Communion, and the Conference commends to the consideration of the Church the suggestions of the Committee on Missionary Problems dealing with this subject which have been made after consultation with experts, and are contained in their Report.

40. Whereas from time to time restrictions on Missionary Freedom have been imposed by Governments, we desire to reaffirm the duty which rests upon every Christian man and woman, of propagating the Faith of Christ, and to claim that any restrictions should be of a strictly temporary nature only, so that freedom of opportunity to fulfil this spiritual obligation may be afforded to Christians of all nationalities.

41. On the subject of the relation of Governments and Government officials to Christianity and other Faiths, the Conference gives its approval to the words used in paragraphs 2 and 3 on page 92 in the Report on Missionary Problems, and commends them to the careful consideration of all concerned.

42. We gratefully acknowledge the valuable work done by British and American Missionary Conferences in safeguarding missionary interests, and believe that such Conferences, both National and International, while claiming no coercive power, have a great part to play in fostering international understanding and goodwill, co-ordinating work, formulating common policies, and serving as a practical medium of communication between Missions and Governments in matters of general Missionary concern.

DEVELOPMENT OF PROVINCES.

43. Whereas it is undesirable that Dioceses should remain indefinitely in isolation or attached only to a distant Province, the gradual creation of new Provinces should be encouraged, and each newly founded Diocese should as soon as possible find its place as a constituent member in some neighbouring Province. The fact that Dioceses proposing to form a Province owe their origin to missions of different Branches of the Anglican Communion need be no bar to such action.

(*a*) In the opinion of the Conference four is the minimum number of Dioceses suitable to form a Province. No number should be considered too great to form a Province, so long as the Bishops and other representatives of the Diocese are able conveniently to meet for mutual consultation and for the transaction of provincial business.

(*b*) In the initiation of any Province in the future, the organization which the Conference deems essential to provincial life is a House or College of Bishops to which the Metropolitans or the Presiding Bishops concerned have conveyed their authority for the consecration of Bishops. It is desirable that when a new Province is formed the Bishops of the constituent Dioceses should transfer their allegiance to the Metropolitan of the Province or other authority constitutionally appointed to receive it, and thereafter all Bishops consecrated for the service of the Province should take the oath of canonical obedience to the Metropolitan or make a declaration of conformity to other authority before mentioned

(c) In newly established Provinces arrangements should be made whereby the Province should have some distinct voice in the election of its Metropolitan.

(d) As to the *sedes* of the Metropolitan customs vary and the decision must depend on local circumstances.

(e) Until a Missionary Diocese becomes largely self-supporting and is self-governed by a Synod the appointment of its Bishop should rest with the Province to which it is attached, after consultation with the Diocese and in such a way as the Province may decide.

(f) A newly constituted Synod of Bishops shall proceed as soon as possible to associate with itself in some official way the clergy and laity of the Province, provided that in the case of Provinces including Missionary Dioceses this procedure shall be subordinate to local circumstances. It is understood that each national and regional Church will determine its own con-stitutional and canonical enactments.

CONSULTATIVE BODY.

44. In order to prevent misapprehension the Conference declares that the Consultative Body, created by the Lambeth Conference of 1897 and consolidated by the Conference of 1908, is a purely advisory Body. It is of the nature of a continuation Committee of the whole Conference and neither possesses nor claims any executive or administrative power. It is framed so as to represent all branches of the Anglican Communion and it offers advice only when advice is asked for.

(a) The existing Consultative Body shall be reconstructed on the following plan of representation :—It shall consist of the Archbishop of Canterbury (*ex-officio*) and of representative Bishops appointed as follows: Province of Canterbury 1, Province of York 1, Province of Wales 1, the Church of Ireland 1, the Episcopal Church in Scotland 1, the Protestant Episcopal Church in the United States of America 4, the Church of England in Canada 1, the Church of England in the Dioceses of Australia and Tasmania 1, the Church of the Province of New Zealand 1, the Church of the Province of the West Indies 1, the Church of the Province of South Africa 1, the Church of the Province of India and Ceylon 1, the Churches in China and Japan and the Diocese of Corea 1, the Missionary and other extra-provincial Bishops under the jurisdiction of the Archbishop of Canterbury 1. Total 18.

(b) The Churches that appoint Representatives shall be free to fix the method of appointment, whether by the House of Bishops or by Synod or Convention. A representative Bishop shall be appointed for a definite term not exceeding six years, and need not be a member of the body which appoints him. Any vacancy by death, resignation, or other cause, during the term of office shall be filled by the Church in the representation of which the vacancy occurs.

(c) For the purpose of appointing the Bishop who is to represent the body of missionary and other extra-provincial Bishops under the jurisdiction of the Archbishop of Canterbury, each of those Bishops shall be requested by the Archbishop of Canterbury to nominate a Bishop to him. The list of Bishops so nominated shall be then sent to all the Bishops entitled to vote, and each of them shall, if he thinks fit to vote, send to the Archbishop the name of the one in that list for whom he votes. The largest number of votes shall carry the election.

(d) The Central Consultative Body shall be prepared to consider questions referred to it by any Bishop, but shall, before considering as well as in considering them, have careful regard to any limitations upon such references as may be imposed by the regulations of Provinces or of national or regional Churches.

(e) The Consultative Body shall not at any meeting come to a decision on any subject not named in the notice summoning the meeting.

45 The Consultative Body is asked to take into its consideration the provisions of the Colonial Clergy Act with a view to their modification.

THE POSITION OF WOMEN IN THE COUNCILS AND MINISTRATIONS OF THE CHURCH.

46. Women should be admitted to those Councils of the Church to which laymen are admitted, and on equal terms. Diocesan, Provincial, or National Synods may decide when or how this principle is to be brought into effect.

47. The time has come when, in the interests of the Church at large, and in particular of the development of the Ministry of

Women, the Diaconate of Women should be restored formally and canonically, and should be recognized throughout the Anglican Communion.

48. The Order of Deaconesses is for women the one and only Order of the Ministry which has the stamp of Apostolic approval, and is for women the only Order of the Ministry which we can recommend that our Branch of the Catholic Church should recognize and use.

49. The office of a Deaconess is primarily a ministry of succour, bodily and spiritual, especially to women, and should follow the lines of the primitive rather than of the modern Diaconate of men. It should be understood that the Deaconess dedicates herself to a lifelong service, but that no vow or implied promise of celibacy should be required as necessary for admission to the Order. Nevertheless, Deaconesses who desire to do so may legitimately pledge themselves either as members of a Community, or as individuals, to a celibate life.

50. In every Branch of the Anglican Communion there should be adopted a Form and Manner of Making of Deaconesses such as might fitly find a place in the Book of Common Prayer, containing in all cases provision for :—

(a) Prayer by the Bishop and the laying on of his hands ;

(b) A formula giving authority to execute the Office of a Deaconess in the Church of God ;

(c) The delivery of the New Testament by the Bishop to each candidate.

51. The Forms for the Making and Ordering of Deaconesses should be of the same general character, and as far as possible similar in their most significant parts, though varying in less important details in accordance with local needs.

52. The following functions may be entrusted to the Deaconess, in addition to the ordinary duties which would naturally fall to her :—

(a) To prepare candidates for Baptism and Confirmation ;

(b) To assist at the administration of Holy Baptism ; and to be the administrant in cases of necessity in virtue of her office ;

(c) To pray with and to give counsel to such women as desire help in difficulties and perplexities.

(d) With the approval of the Bishop and of the Parish Priest, and under such conditions as shall from time to time be laid down by the Bishop : (i) in Church to read Morning and Evening

Prayer and the Litany, except such portions as are assigned to the Priest only ; (ii) in Church also to lead in prayer and, under licence of the Bishop, to instruct and exhort the Congregation.

[*Note.*—Clause *d* (ii) was carried by 117 votes to 81.]

53. Opportunity should be given to women as to men (duly qualified and approved by the Bishop) to speak in consecrated or unconsecrated buildings, and to lead in prayer, at other than the regular and appointed services of the Church. Such diocesan arrangements, both for men and for women, should wherever possible be subject to Provincial control and co-ordination.

54. The Conference recommends that careful inquiry should be made in the several branches of the Anglican Communion as to the position and recognition of women workers in the Church, the conditions of their employment, and the remuneration of those who receive salaries.

SPIRITUALISM, CHRISTIAN SCIENCE, THEOSOPHY.

55. We reaffirm our conviction that the revelation of God in Christ Jesus is the supreme and sufficient message given to all mankind, whereby we may attain to eternal life. We recognize that modern movements of thought connected with Spiritualism, Christian Science, and Theosophy join with the Christian Church in protesting against a materialistic view of the universe and at some points emphasize partially neglected aspects of truth. At the same time, we feel bound to call attention to the fact that both in the underlying philosophy and in cults and practices which have arisen out of these movements, the teaching given or implied either ignores or explains away or contradicts the unique and central fact of human history, namely, the Incarnation of our Lord and Saviour Jesus Christ.

56. We recognize that new phenomena of consciousness have been presented to us, which claim, and at the hands of competent psychologists have received, careful investigation, and, as far as possible, the application of scientific method. But such scientific researches have confessedly not reached an advanced stage, and we are supported by the best psychologists in warning our people against accepting as final theories which further knowledge may disprove, and still more against the indiscriminate and undisciplined exercise of psychic powers, and the habit of recourse to *séances*, " seers," and mediums.

Spiritualism.

57. The Conference, while prepared to expect and welcome new light from psychical research upon the powers and processes of the spirit of man, urges strongly that a larger place should be given in the teaching of the Church to the explanation of the true grounds of Christian belief in eternal life, and in immortality, and of the true content of belief in the Communion of Saints as involving real fellowship with the departed through the love of God in Christ Jesus.

58. The Conference, while recognizing that the results of investigation have encouraged many people to find a spiritual meaning and purpose in human life and led them to believe in survival after death, sees grave dangers in the tendency to make a religion of spiritualism. The practice of spiritualism as a cult involves the subordination of the intelligence and the will to unknown forces or personalities and, to that extent, an abdication of the self-control to which God has called us. It tends to divert attention from the approach to God through the one Mediator, Jesus Christ, under the guidance of the Holy Spirit; to ignore the discipline of faith as the path of spiritual training; and to depreciate the divinely ordained channels of grace and truth revealed and given through Jesus Christ our Lord.

Christian Science.

59. The Conference finds that while Christian Science fixes attention on the supremacy of spirit, yet in the teaching given there is a direct tendency (*a*) to pantheistic doctrine, and at the same time (*b*) to a false antithesis between spirit and matter, and (*c*) to the denial of the reality of sin, and (*d*) to the denial of the reality of disease and suffering. Such teaching, therefore, cannot be reconciled with the fundamental truths of the Christian Faith and the teaching of Scripture on atonement, penitence, forgiveness, and fellowship in the sufferings of Christ.

60. The Conference reminds the Church that intimate communion with God has been the privilege and joy of the Saints in every age. This communion, realised in union with Christ through the Holy Spirit, influences the whole personality of man, physical and spiritual, enabling him to share his Lord's triumph over sin, disease and death.

61. We therefore urge upon the clergy of the Anglican Communion the duty of a more thorough study of the many-sided enterprise of prayer in order that they may become more efficient teachers and trainers of their people in this work, so that through the daily practice of prayer and meditation the corporate faith of the Church may be renewed, and the fruit of the Spirit may be more manifest in the daily lives of professing Christians, and the power of Christ to heal may be released.

62. We declare our thankfulness for the devoted labours of those engaged in scientific research and for the progress made in medicine, surgery, nursing, hygiene and sanitation. Believing that all these means of healing and preventing disease and removing suffering are gifts that come from God, we acknowledge our duty to use them faithfully for the welfare of mankind.

63. For the general guidance of the Church the Conference requests the Archbishop of Canterbury to appoint a Committee to consider and report as early as possible upon the use with prayer of the laying on of hands, of the unction of the sick and other spiritual means of healing, the findings of such a Committee to be reported forthwith to the authorities of the national, provincial and regional Churches of the Anglican Communion.

Theosophy.

64. The Conference, while recognizing that the three publicly stated objects of the Theosophical Society (see Report, p. 126) do not in themselves appear to be inconsistent with loyal membership of the Church, desires to express its conviction that there are cardinal elements in the positive teaching current in theosophical circles and literature which are irreconcilable with the Christian faith as to the Person and mission of Christ and with the missionary claim and duty of the Christian religion as the message of God to all mankind. The Conference warns Christian people who may be induced to make a study of theosophy by the seemingly Christian elements contained in it to be on their guard against the ultimate bearing of theosophical teaching, and urges them to examine strictly the character and credentials of the teachers upon whose authority they are encouraged or compelled to rely.

65. The Conference, believing that the attraction of Theosophy for some Christian people lies largely in its presentation of Christian faith as a quest for knowledge, recommends that in the current teaching of the Church due regard should be given to the mystical elements of faith and life which underlie the historic belief of Christendom, and on the other hand urges all thinking people to safeguard their Christian position by a fuller study of the Bible, Creed, and Sacraments in the light of sound Christian scholarship and philosophy.

PROBLEMS OF MARRIAGE AND SEXUAL MORALITY.

66. Recognizing that to live a pure and chaste life before and after marriage is, for both sexes, the unchangeable Christian standard, attainable and attained through the help of the Holy Spirit by men and women in every age, the Conference desires to proclaim the universal obligation of this standard, and its vital importance as an essential condition of human happiness.

67. The Conference affirms as our Lord's principle and standard of marriage a life-long and indissoluble union, for better for worse, of one man with one woman, to the exclusion of all others on either side, and calls on all Christian people to maintain and bear witness to this standard.

Nevertheless, the Conference admits the right of a national or regional Church within our Communion to deal with cases which fall within the exception mentioned in the record of our Lord's words in St. Matthew's Gospel, under provisions which such Church may lay down

The Conference, while fully recognizing the extreme difficulty of governments in framing marriage laws for citizens many of whom do not accept the Christian standard, expresses its firm belief that in every country the Church should be free to bear witness to that standard through its powers of administration and discipline exercised in relation to its own members.

68. The Conference, while declining to lay down rules which will meet the needs of every abnormal case, regards with grave concern the spread in modern society of theories and practices hostile to the family. We utter an emphatic warning against the use of unnatural means for the avoidance of conception, together with the grave dangers—physical, moral, and religious—thereby incurred, and against the evils with which the extension of such use threatens the race. In opposition to the teaching which, under the name of science and religion, encourages married people in the deliberate cultivation of sexual union as an end in itself, we steadfastly uphold what must always be regarded as the governing considerations of Christian marriage. One is the primary purpose for which marriage exists, namely the continuation of the race through the gift and heritage of children; the other is the paramount importance in married life of deliberate and thoughtful self-control.

We desire solemnly to commend what we have said to Christian people and to all who will hear.

69. The Conference, moved by responsible statements from many nations as to the prevalence of venereal diseases, bringing suffering, paralysis, insanity, or death to many thousands of the innocent as well as the guilty, supports all efforts which are consistent with high moral standards to check the causes of the diseases and to treat and, if possible, cure the victims. We impress upon the clergy and members of the Church the duty of joining with physicians and public authorities in meeting this scourge, and urge the clergy to guide those who turn to them for advice with knowledge, sympathy, and directness. The Conference must condemn the distribution or use, before exposure to infection, of so-called prophylactics, since these cannot but be regarded as an invitation to vice.

70. The Conference urges the importance of enlisting the help of all high-principled men and women, whatever be their religious beliefs, in co-operation with or, if necessary, in bringing pressure to bear upon, authorities both national and local, for removing such incentives to vice as indecent literature, suggestive plays and films, the open or secret sale of contraceptives, and the continued existence of brothels.

71. With regard to the education of the young in matters of sex, the Conference presses upon parents that the duty of giving right teaching on these subjects rests primarily with them, and that it is the duty of all persons giving such instruction to prepare themselves for this responsible task. Boys and girls should be guarded against the danger of acquiring knowledge of sexual subjects from wrong persons and in wrong ways.

72. Bearing in remembrance the example of our Lord, and the prominent place that He gave in His ministry to protecting the weak and raising the fallen, the Conference deplores the common apathy of Church people in regard to Preventive and Rescue Work, and urges on Bishops, Clergy, and all Christian people the duty of taking a more active share in this essential part of the Church's life

---

SOCIAL AND INDUSTRIAL QUESTIONS.

73. We desire to emphasize our conviction that the pursuit of mere self-interest, whether individual or corporate, will never bring healing to the wounds of Society. This conviction is at once exemplified and reinforced by what has happened in and since the War. Nor is this less true when that self-interest is equipped with every advantage of science and education. Our only hope lies in reverent allegiance to the Person of Christ, whose Law is the Law of Love, in acceptance of His principles, and reliance on His power.

74. An outstanding and pressing duty of the Church is to convince its members of the necessity of nothing less than a fundamental change in the spirit and working of our economic life. This change can only be effected by accepting as the basis of industrial relations the principle of co-operation in service for the common good in place of unrestricted competition for private or sectional advantage. All Christian people ought to take an active part in bringing about this change, by which alone we can hope to remove class dissensions and ⌐resolve industrial discords.

75. The Church cannot in its corporate capacity be an advocate or partisan, " a judge or a divider," in political or class disputes where moral issues are not at stake : nevertheless even in matters of economic and political controversy the Church is bound to give its positive and active corporate witness to the Christian principles of justice, brotherhood, and the equal and infinite value of every human personality.

76. In obedience to Christ's teaching as to covetousness and self-seeking, the Conference calls upon all members of His Church to be foremost both by personal action and sacrifice in maintaining the superiority of the claims of human life to those of property. To this end it would emphasize the duty which is laid upon all Christians of setting human values above dividends and profits in their conduct of business, of avoiding extravagance and waste, and⌐ of upholding a high standard of honour and thoroughness in work. In a word, they must set an example in subordinating the claim for rights to the call of duty.

77. Members of the Church are bound to take an active part, by public action and by personal service, in removing those abuses which depress and impoverish human life. In company with other citizens and organizations they should work for reform, and particularly for such measures as will secure the better care of children, including real opportunity for an adequate education ; protection of the workers against unemployment ; and the provision of healthy homes.

78. The Church is bound to use its influence to remove inhuman or oppressive conditions of labour in all parts of the world, especially among the weaker races, and to give its full support to those clauses in the League of Nations Covenant which aim at raising by international agreement the status of industrial workers in all countries.

79. The Conference notes with deep interest the prohibition by the will of the people of the sale and manufacture of intoxicating drinks in the Republic of the United States of America, and of their sale in most of the Provinces of Canada, and commends this action to the earnest and sympathetic attention of the Christian Church throughout the world. The Conference urges members of the Church in other countries—

(1) To support such legislation as will lead to a speedy reduction in the use of intoxicants ;

(2) To recognize the duty of combating the evil of intemperance by personal example and willing self-sacrifice.

80. If the Church is to witness without reproach for justice and brotherhood in the world, it must shew itself serious and insistent in reforming abuses within its own organization, and in promoting brotherhood among its own members. Further, if Christian witness is to be fully effective it must be borne by nothing short of the whole body of Christian people.

N.B.—*The following Reports must be taken as having the authority only of the Committees by whom they were respectively prepared and presented. The Committees were not in every case unanimous in adopting the Reports.*

The Conference, as a whole, is responsible only for the formal Resolutions agreed to after discussion, and printed above.

** *An asterisk placed after the name of any Member of Committee denotes that he was unable to attend any of the Meetings of that Committee.*

REPORT OF THE COMMITTEE† APPOINTED TO CONSIDER AND
REPORT UPON THE SUBJECT OF CHRISTIANITY AND
INTERNATIONAL RELATIONS, ESPECIALLY THE LEAGUE OF
NATIONS.

WE are in no doubt as to the main tenor of our message.
Humanity has suffered long years, and, for all its expenditure
of blood and treasure, has been "nothing bettered," but is
rather grown worse, and is now feeling dimly for the hem of His
garment by whose power alone it may be made whole. One
by one our human expedients have failed. Defensive arma-
ments on the principle *si vis pacem, para bellum,* alliances
to secure the balance of power, the efforts of noble minded
diplomatists through the concert of Europe, and the far-seeing
pronouncements of experts in international law, all have contributed their quota, but the world's wound is not healed, and
now the League of Nations—the latest and greatest of all human
expedients—is painfully struggling into life What is the moral
of all this ? The moral is that the social order for which
humanity hungers is beyond the reach of merely human expedients.
Nothing will establish peace on the earth but a new creation
from God in response to repentance and prayer.

At the present moment there are two alternatives before the
world. On the one hand we may relapse into the old conditions,
with an attempted balance of power, and the piling up of arma-
ments with their attendant expenditure, until the world is ready
for another and even more hideous war. On the other hand,
we may work for the ideal for mankind which shines before us
in the pages of the New Testament, guided by the principles
which we have learnt from the Lord Jesus Christ.

† Names of Members of the Committee :—

Bishop of Aberdeen*	Bishop of Mombasa*
Bishop of Adelaide.	Bishop of Natal
Bishop in Argentina.	Bishop of New Westminster.
Bishop of Arizona.	Bishop of North Carolina.
Archbishop of Brisbane (*Chairman*).	Bishop of Southern Rhodesia*
Bishop of Connecticut.	Archbishop of Nova Scotia.
Bishop in Corea*	Bishop Oluwole.
Bishop of Durham.	Bishop of Oxford.
Bishop of George.	Bishop Roach (Natal Assistant
Bishop of Kalgoorlie*	Bishop).
Bishop of Kampala (*Secretary*)	Bishop of Sodor and Man
Bishop of Kimberley.	Bishop of Southwell
Bishop of Kwangsi.	Bishop of Washington.
Bishop of Lichfield	Archbishop of West Indies.
Bishop of Lincoln*	Bishop of Winchester.
Bishop of Maryland	Bishop of Worcester.
Bishop of Massachusetts.	Bishop of Zanzibar.

I

The Divine Purpose.

The ideal for human life hangs before Christian eyes in the form of a perfect city through whose ever-open gates the nations and their rulers bring their several distinctive contributions of strength or beauty. The Vision of the Apocalypse sets before us the ultimate consummation in the mind of God of the spiritual development of the nations. In the City of God there is no merging of individuality in a common impersonal existence. Not only the individual, but the nations, will there realize themselves and achieve maturity. The glory of the Kingdom will be the sum total of the glory of the nations, not some new thing in which the nations will be submerged and disappear. " The kings of the earth do bring their glory and honour into it." And, again, the nations of the earth will enter upon this full spiritual maturity in proportion as they rise out of the self-seeking, the pride, the avarice, the dishonesty which at present stain political relations. " There shall in no wise enter into it anything that defileth or maketh a lie "

This may seem an elusive conception, but it is essential that all who are working for the world's progress—the statesmen, the teachers, the leaders of commerce—should take hold of the ideal, not as opportunists, but as master-builders, working to a divine plan.

The principles of true progress, imperfectly recognized in all higher morality, are brought into simplicity, coherence and fulness in Jesus Christ. They are disclosed in His precepts, and embodied in His example : " Thou shalt love thy neighbour as thyself." The law of unselfish human neighbourliness is expressly declared as fundamental. It gives the principle which must be applied to all human relations. Three applications of it stand out as germane to the subject before us

(1) First, there is the duty and dignity of service, and the consequent responsibility of the nations for the service of each other and of the whole " He that is great " is to be "as he that doth serve." The Son of Man came as he that serveth. It follows that a nation's chiefest claim to greatness is its con-sciousness of a mission to humanity Not in domination, but in service, not in will-to-power, but in will-to-help, not in exploita-tion, but in trusteeship, lies the true objective of a great nation

(2) Closely connected with this is another cardinal principle expressed in the Apostolic words :—" Ye are members one of another " It is our Christian duty to recognize that already all the nations, advanced or backward, child races or ancient civilizations, are each of them children in the great family of God. Statesmen thinking for their nation no less than individuals must lay hold of the truth that we are members one of another,

and that no national policy can be Christian which ignores the needs and rightful claims of other nations. Neither markets nor territory nor cheap labour must in the future dictate national policy, but only the principles of justice, and the rights of all. If we really want peace we must set our faces decisively against the vested interests which have so often in the past stood behind governments, and vitiated their action.

(3) A third principle is that which comes direct from our Lord's treatment of the child and of the little one. With even fierce emphasis He warns us against the misuse of strength. " Take heed that ye despise not one of these little ones . . . It were better for him that a millstone were hanged about his neck, and that he were cast into the depths of the sea." This bears with unmistakeable clearness upon the relations of the stronger races to those that are weaker and more backward. And we note with thankfulness that the trend of public opinion has of late set strongly against the exploitation of the weaker races in the interests of the strong. But this responsibility of strong nations involves more than the mere provision of safeguards against wrong : it includes the sympathetic encouragement of those instincts of nationhood which appear as soon as young nations emerge from infancy. The desire to escape from tutelage and to develop individuality denotes a genuine growth towards a fuller life, and to oppose or ignore this instinct, is to incur danger : the road to inter-nationalism, as it has been well said, " lies through nationalism." But it is well to remember that as the consummation of individu-ality is found in the corporate life, so the full development of nationhood is contingent upon the acceptance of international obligations. True nationalism and a keen sense of international responsibility are in truth indispensable correlatives.

In these three applications of the law of love may be seen the duty of the nations in their progress towards the City of God ; and lest any should suppose that these ideas are Utopian, it is well to point out that the ultimate force, in the last analysis, is not physical, but moral. We all know the common belief that it is the big battalions that have their way. No assertion can be more baseless. The progress of the world has usually been in spite of big battalions, and " nothing is ever settled until it is settled right." We look forward to the day when war between nations will be unthinkable, precisely as duels have become unthinkable in civilized society, because public opinion will not tolerate these absurd and horrible ways of settling disputes. Let us not forget the lesson of the last six years The nation that had the best trained army in Europe has been defeated. The nation that was richest in munitions of war has lost, because against her were the moral forces of civilization.

II.

THE LEAGUE OF NATIONS.*

In the League of Nations we have an instrument in the application of these great principles, which all Christians should welcome with both hands.

It is no fruit of a sudden impulse · it is strictly in the line of historical development, and crowns the efforts of nations and statesmen from Hugo Grotius to the Hague Conference of 1907. Before we go further, however, it is worth while to remark that its normal and fundamental purpose cannot be fulfilled till normal conditions are restored. It exists in time of peace to prevent war ; but we do not yet live in times of peace. We may group the clauses of the Covenant of the League under two great heads—those which provide (to quote from the preamble of the Covenant) for the promotion of " international peace and security," and those which provide for " international co-operation " for the safe-guarding of the weak. It is obvious that both these great objectives are based upon the Christian principles already enunciated.

(1) If the clauses aiming at the prevention of war are not to be a dead letter, we must preach with all our power, in season and out of season, in the drawing-room and in the market-place, in the workshop and in the club, the wickedness of hatred. This at the moment is the most appalling barrier in the way of the League of Nations. In every country at the present time the spirit of hatred is at work. Even among the most Christian of our people we find it active beneath the surface and colouring men's attitude. In many cases this spirit is naked and unashamed, and sings its songs of hatred in fierce defiance ; but it is most dangerous when it seems to those who entertain it to be the expression of righteous indignation. They are honestly afraid of ceasing to be angry from mere indolence and indifference. They remember the wickedness and cruelties, and fear lest the world should grow corrupt by loss of a righteous zeal against them In some cases it is injuries done to other nations and not their own which they want not to forget.

A great responsibility rests in this matter with the Press ; for the maintenance or the discouragement of hatred lies mainly there.

We must face the facts. If we wish, whether nation or individual, to enjoy the luxury of hatred, we must pay the price, and the price is another and far more hideous war as soon as ever the nations have sufficiently recovered from their present exhaustion. The very horror of the thought should give us pause :

* The American Bishops of the Committee are cordially agreed in the principle of a League of Nations, but feel obliged to withhold their support of the existing Covenant without certain reservations.

one would think that the inevitable consequences would frighten men out of their hatred; but we should prefer to take higher ground than this. The whole spirit is an utter denial of our Christian calling. We must choose between the spirit of hatred and the spirit of the Lord's Prayer. Is Christendom really so utterly bankrupt of the spirit of Christ?

As a practical example of our duty in this matter, it is incumbent on all Christian people to press for the admission of Germany and other nations into the League at the very earliest moment that the conditions render it possible.

(2) In the mandatory clauses of the Covenant, we see not only an application of Christ's injunction to safeguard the weak, but also a new instrument of unprecedented power for securing justice by international consent. Whatever be the difficulties in the way of effective operation on the political side, the League has already shewn abundant promise in this matter of promoting common international interests. A conspicuous instance of this is the international labour organization in connection with the League. We understand on good authority that this body has accomplished more in eight months for the regulation and betterment of industrial conditions than had been accomplished in years by the old methods of dealing with international affairs. This opens out vistas of hope in other directions. For instance, in China the old abuse of the opium traffic has of late been revived, though morphia is substituted for opium.* The sale of arms and liquor to native races, and still more urgently, the White Slave traffic, have occupied and baffled the energies of philanthropists for years past. In all these great international moral interests any progress made has been mainly, if not entirely,

* The importance of the subject of opium and other habit-forming drugs is evidenced by the place it occupies in the Covenant of the League of Nations, and the text of the Treaty of Peace. Art. 23 (c) of the Covenant deals with it in common with the traffic in women and children. Art. 295 of the Treaty, referring to the Opium Convention of 1912 and the Special Protocol of 1914, provides that ratification of the Treaty involves ratification of the Convention and Protocol. In the meantime, through failure specifically of Great Britain, the United States of America, and Japan, morphia, chiefly of European and American manufacture, is going into China in increasing quantity. The figures given by Dr. Wu Lien-Teh in his article on the " Latest Phase of the Narcotic Problem," in the *Peking and Tientsin Times* of April 5th, 1920, are as follows :

1911	..	..	..	.	..	..	$5\frac{1}{4}$ tons
1912	..	..	..	.	..	..	$7\frac{1}{2}$,,
1913	..	..	..	..	..	..	$11\frac{1}{4}$,,
1914	..	..	..	.	..	.	14 ,,
1915	..	..	..	.	..	..	16 ,,
1916	..	..	.	..	..	..	16 ,,
1917	..	..	..	..	..	..	$22\frac{1}{4}$,,
1918	..	..	..	.	..	..	$22\frac{1}{2}$,,
1919	..	..	.	..	..	..	28 ,,

Immediate and drastic measures should be taken by the governments concerned to bring to a speedy end so shameful a condition of affairs.

due to the initiative and pressure of religious organizations.
In the face of great inertia, conventions and conferences have
been held, although, in consequence perhaps of inadequate method,
they have not proved very effective. The organizations under
the League will not only provide a vastly superior machinery,
but the moral influence of the nations behind them will be a
guarantee that the findings of future conferences will be effectively
carried out In one direction, especially, we look to the future
with eager hope. All over the world, and especially in South
and East Africa, questions are arising through the conflicting
interests of native races and white settlers. It is obvious to the
Christian conscience that full justice must be done to the natives
in regard to both the tenure of land and to any employment of
their labour which involves virtual slavery. We welcome in
this connexion the clear statement of the Secretary of State for the
Colonies in the House of Lords on July 14th, 1920, that except
for certain specified purposes of genuinely public utility, " it is
illegal to use force to procure labour in our East African possessions
for any purpose whatever " Yet the temptation is still with
us to confiscate the land, and to enslave the labour of the native
races. The principle of the League involves an absolutely equal
claim to justice for the natives and ourselves before the recognized
tribunal, and, with all Christians whose consciences have been
troubled by what we cannot help calling the shifty policy of
governments in these matters, we hail the League of Nations,
with its mandatory principles, as the very ally for which, in the
past, we have looked and longed in vain.

III.

The Immediate Situation.

WE turn from the bright future to the situation of to-day
It is useless to shut our eyes to the fact that, judged by the
measure of public interest, the League of Nations is as yet only
hovering on the verge of existence. The smaller nations, it is
true, shew eagerness ; but this can hardly be said of the governments of the great nations, either in Europe or elsewhere. Russia
is still an unknown quantity , America hesitates ; and Germany
is still outside. While individual statesmen are working with
noble zeal and devotion, it is obvious that the task is too great
for them, unless they can count upon the full support of the
spiritual forces of civilization.

How can we get to work ? First, we shall press for a fair
trial of the League itself—for its practical inauguration to the
fullest extent. It is becoming clear, even to the outsider, that
there are imperfections in the machinery of the Covenant ; and
this lays the nations open to a natural temptation to ignore it
and seek a solution of difficulties along other channels. Let us
frankly face the possibility that the machinery may require

amendment ; for nothing could be worse than the perpetuation of an instrument to which everyone would pay homage, but which in practice would only be a cover for decisions reached by other means.

Meanwhile our own immediate duty is to press for an active propaganda throughout the world. Everywhere we meet with much ignorance and indifference, and there is not a little reasoned scepticism. These obstacles must be overcome ; and the first necessity is a campaign of education throughout the British Commonwealth and the Republic of the United States, for which we must claim all the collective movements of our time making for genuine internationalism.

(1) Ready to hand is the League of Nations Union, the recognized organization for the propaganda of the League which should have in every place the Church's active co-operation and support. From this Union we shall ask for literature of an educational kind, books on international questions for study circles, schemes of intercession, and administrative methods whereby branches shall be systematically formed throughout the world and their leaders kept in close touch with headquarters.

(2) We shall claim in the next place the co-operation and practical ability of those who form in each free nation so large a section of the people, the organized workers themselves   " The project of the League of Nations," as one of their own leaders has just said, " is the keystone of the new social order that nations desire to build "   In the International Labour Conference set up in connexion with the League of Nations 41 nations are already represented And already practical issues are within sight. For instance, if the proposals of the Washington Conference (November 1919) are carried into effect, the result will be that in Japan child-labour below the age of 14 will be prohibited, a weekly rest-day established, and the working-day reduced from 11 to 9½ hours.

(3) Further organizations are the International Chamber of Commerce, and the Institute for International Affairs In connexion with the first of these, representative business men from the leading nations are seeking to restore normal conditions, to obviate friction, to foster trade between the various nations In the Institute is to be welcomed a valuable centre for the interchange of precise knowledge between leaders' of public opinion, with a view to a constructive policy in international affairs.

Beside those of a more political and economic character, we look with hope to two definitely spiritual movements.

(4) The World Alliance for Promoting International Friendship through the Churches is one of them Though temporarily hindered by the war, this Alliance is now developing rapidly, and in the Conference to be held in Geneva in August 1920 the representatives of twenty nations are expected : it may well grow into a potent ally of the League of Nations Union on the spiritual side.

(5) The other movement is that world-wide organisation of young men and women, the impressive significance of which is not yet, we believe, sufficiently understood The Student Christian Movement, touching, as it does, the students of all nations at an impressionable time, may become a mighty instrument for propagating the spirit of peace. Already the Universities and Colleges of forty States are represented in it. The youth of the nations is streaming through its gates, and at any given moment the membership may be reckoned at 200,000

But in all propaganda we must clearly begin with ourselves. We must seek in ourselves and in our fellow Christians a re-adjustment of our ideas for the extension of Christ's Kingdom, and learn to preach the cause of a worldwide good-will as we preach the cause of a worldwide gospel In our Church Assem-blies and Councils, whether National, Provincial, Diocesan or Parochial, internationalism must take its place as an integral part of the Kingdom of Christ which we stand to promote.

The work of propaganda is comparatively easy. More difficult is it to meet the scepticism of practical men who see the undoubted dangers which must ever beset leadership in the cause of peace There are those who say that in taking up mandates all over the world the British Commonwealth is exposing herself in a score of vulnerable places to the machina-tions of dangerous political agents. Again, they note that so far Britain is almost alone in the offering of men and money for the police work of the League ; and again there is a danger at home in the impatience of those who press for immediate disarmament without reference to the facts of the situation. We do not in the least minimize these dangers, but we appeal to all those who are held back by these or kindred scruples, to view the matter in the Christian way, and to have the courage of faith. If peace is to be achieved, risks must be taken. Most of us decided when the war broke out that it is not God's will that we should break up society by laying down our arms and refusing the responsibilities of war. But our very decision should make us more alert to discern where risks should legitimately be taken. We believe that in supporting the League of Nations, we are called upon to take the risks involved in a frank and open policy of peace. We believe that a bold venture of faith will rally to the League all the unmeasured forces of goodwill which are latent in the nations of the earth.

There is, in our judgement, no other way. The course we urge is a course based upon repentance for the past and bold faith in the call of God's Spirit for the future. If penitence and faith be found in the earth, then the materials will be there for that new creation from God which is the one hope of a corrupt and stricken world.

(Signed) ST. CLAIR BRISBANE,

Chairman.

No. II.

REPORT OF THE COMMITTEE† APPOINTED TO CONSIDER THE OPPORTUNITY AND DUTY OF THE CHURCH IN REGARD TO INDUSTRIAL AND SOCIAL PROBLEMS.

I.

THE OPPORTUNITY.

THE difficulty of this present time is the measure of the Church's opportunity It is part of the heritage of war that our social and industrial problems should press upon us with redoubled insistence. But the turmoil among the nations has opened to the Church a door of witness and of service.

(1) The war shewed us the inevitable result of the attempt to build up civilization on selfishness and force The doctrine that national power is an end in itself, and that self-interest

† Names of Members of the Committee :—

Bishop of Adelaide	Bishop of Nebraska
Bishop of Antigua	Bishop of Newark
Bishop of Auckland	Bishop of Newcastle (N.S W.)
Bishop of Barking	Bishop of North Queensland
Bishop of Bradford	Bishop of Olympia*
Bishop of Buckingham	Bishop of Ontario*
Bishop of Calcutta*	Bishop of Persia
Bishop of Cashel	Bishop of Peterborough
Bishop of Chelmsford*	Bishop of Riverina
Bishop of Coventry	Bishop of Rockhampton
Bishop Crossley	Bishop of St Albans
Bishop of Croydon	Bishop of St. Andrews*
Bishop of Dover	Bishop of St. Edmundsbury
Bishop of Fredericton	Bishop of Sheffield
Bishop Garland	Bishop of South Carolina
Bishop of Glasgow	Bishop of Stepney (*Secretary*)
Bishop of Huron	Bishop of Swansea
Bishop of Jarrow	Bishop of Tasmania
Bishop of Kansas*	Bishop of Tennessee*
Bishop of Lichfield (*Chairman*)	Bishop of Toronto
Bishop of Maine	Bishop of Tuam
Bishop of Michigan	Bishop of Warrington
Bishop of Milwaukee	Bishop of Willesden
Bishop Nash (Capetown Coadjutor)	Bishop of Woolwich

is the ruling principle of political life, could only lead to war. The great prophet of that false doctrine was Germany ; but who shall say that it was wholly repudiated by the other nations of the world ? Now a similar doctrine has dominated a great part of our industrial system. It has been commonly held that different individuals, different sections or interests or classes, must pursue their own self-interest, and that the result of that pursuit would be the best possible condition of society as a whole. Experience has shewn that this doctrine is false. Where there has been a conflict of interests the issue has been determined by a mere trial of force, instead of by a consideration of what is just between man and man. The result has been a war spirit in industry corresponding to a war spirit among the nations. Our experience of the past five years has led us to the determination that this war spirit shall be cast out. Such a spirit is equally disastrous in the capitalist, who is determined at all costs to maintain the controlling power of capital, and in the disciple of Marx, who preaches " class war " and wishes violently to " expropriate the expropriator." As we desire a League of Nations which shall unite the peoples in a fellowship for the common good, so we look for some means of co-operation within the nation, which by ways of liberty and justice shall transcend all class distinctions, and enable all to make their contribution of service for the welfare of all.

(2) To such a union of goodwill we looked forward when in the stress of war we were forming high hopes for a better and happier order in the days of peace. The sense of national unity against a common foe warranted the hope of a like unity of purpose in making war on misery, poverty, and discord, the common foes of all human life. In the fellowship of the trenches men learned to recognize that no section of the community is wholly bad or wholly good, but that each possesses to a large extent the same good qualities and failings. There was ground for hope that, in their appreciation of the value of fellowship, men would come to loathe the antagonisms of class warfare, and would do their utmost to remove the causes which led to it. Again, the spirit of self-sacrifice, shewn on so wide a scale and in so noble a way by rich and poor alike, taught us afresh that when the right appeal is made, the hearts of men will respond to the call to venture life itself in the cause of justice. Can we believe that the increase of these good fruits of co-operation, comradeship, and sacrifice has been choked by the poisonous aftermath of war ? May we not dare to hope that, given the right aim, they will even yet be found abundantly on the side of right in the effort to ameliorate the industrial conditions of our time ?

With regard to our general outlook on the future, it may be that there was too much thought of merely material prosperity. But, in the main, our aspirations were sound and true.

If the Church is bound to contend that the first things, which are spiritual, must come first, its members must not forget that Our Lord, who won His victory in the spiritual sphere, intended that victory to cover the whole of life : an applied Christianity must shew the Gospel everywhere in action If we keep the right aim in view we shall seek to make the outward order of society an embodiment of Christian justice and love. No one could say that this is the character of the social and industrial state of Christendom to-day

(3) What then is the right aim ? The trial of these six years has helped us to the true answer. No self-regarding purpose will suffice a self-centred individual security or a Church-centred corporate selfishness is equally insufficient : the individual and the Church find themselves when they lose themselves in their ultimate aim, " Seek ye first the Kingdom of God and His righteousness " Any definition of the Kingdom of God must assuredly contain the ideal of " human life according to God's intention " It must include the extension everywhere of the knowledge of God's sovereignty of love, and the claim that His sovereign sway shall govern every part of life : the former is the missionary work of the Church, the latter is the witness of the Church concerning social and industrial righteousness

We do not for a moment deny that the primary business of the Church is to deal with the individual. Personal relationship with God in Christ is vital religion, and without personal conversion our labour will be vain. But we want the conversion to be real and complete. The converted life is Christ-centred, not self-centred ; it means the acceptance of Christ as King And if He is King anywhere, He must be King everywhere. He cannot be excluded from politics, or industry, or from any of our social relationships. His Kingdom is not of this world, but it finds its expression often in material things. No Christian writer has pleaded more earnestly than Bishop Westcott for the supremacy of the spiritual. He warned us to distinguish between life and the mere means of living , he declared that the Nineteenth century attached an unnatural and abnormal importance to material wealth. Yet he also wrote, " every amelioration of the outward conditions of men's lives is the translation of a fragment of our Creed into action." We are convinced that the Gospel of the Kingdom includes a social message

Such a conviction must be borne in on all who consider Our Lord's Person, and study the record of His teaching and His work When He, the eternal Son of God, took our complete human nature He shewed us that nothing human is alien to the mind of God. He entered into and shared all human experience—except the sin which He came to take away He worked as a carpenter at Nazareth. When, during His ministry,

He went about doing good, He cared for the bodies as well as the souls of men   He came that men might have life and have it abundantly : life at its highest is the eternal life which is fellowship with God, but all that belongs to man's best activities and truest affections comes within the scope of His purpose. His teaching shews the large humanness of His sympathy.   The farmer in his fields, the shepherd with his flock, the housewife in her home, the business man with his trade in pearls, and the children playing in the streets—He knew and cared for them all.   While it would be unwise to press the details of a parable, the story of the labourers in the vineyard, alluding as it does to the problems of unemployment, thoroughness in work and a living wage, shews how sure was His touch on the labour questions of His day.   Our Lord was much more than a social reformer, for He went down to the root of all human life, and those who learn His measure of values, and follow His path of service in the power of His Life, are the men who will transform the world.

Before we consider more fully the message of Christ and try to formulate the Church's duty in these matters, it will be necessary to review some of the special features of the present situation.

II.

SPECIAL FEATURES OF THE SITUATION.

1. *The Labour Movement.*

What shall we say of the relation of the Church to the Labour Movement, which is one of the outstanding factors in the industrial world ?   We cannot claim a good record with regard to labour questions.   Since the beginning of the industrial revolution only a minority of the members of our Church have insisted on the social application of the Gospel   Now that the conscience of the Christian community has been stirred, we must be content to bear the accusation that we are only trying to make ourselves popular with labour, because labour is now a dominant power.   The accusation is not true.   We are honestly trying to see and to speak the truth, and those who make that effort will not, in the long run, be popular with any party.   The question is not whether labour is friendly to the Church, or whether we can attract labour men to the Church, but whether the ideals of labour are sound and its claims just.   No doubt there are strata in the labour movement, as in "the world" generally, which are secularist and materialistic.   Certainly, also, there are labour men (though not so many in the English-speaking peoples as on the continent of Europe) who are advocates of violent revolution.   But we ought, in all fairness, to judge the labour movement at its best, and to consider what is to be the relation of its idealism to the idealism of the Church. The purpose of the labour movement, at its best, is to secure fulness of life, the opportunity of a complete development of their manhood and womanhood for those who labour, it seeks to furnish a better world for people to live in. While this is also the Church's aim, our supreme task must be to provide better people to live in the world. The labour movement can help the Church by bringing us into touch with actualities, and increasing our discontent with mere pious aspirations; and assuredly the Church can help the labour movement by pointing the way to that spiritual power which alone can bring the law of righteousness and love into permanent action. " He who can spiritualize democracy," said Mazzini, " will save the world."

It must not be inferred from these references to the labour movement that we fail to recognize other efforts for the promotion of a better social order. There are many men and women in all classes of society whose self-sacrificing service is bearing good fruit. And there are captains of industry who are prepared to welcome a complete change in the existing scheme. Mr. W. L. Hichens (chairman of Cammell, Laird and Co.) has said : " No tinkering scheme of piecemeal reform will avail to cure our ills ; the light must be let in on all dark places at once ; the muddy pools of class selfishness must be cleansed ; the self-sacrifice of our soldiers and sailors must find its counterpart in our industrial life."

2. *International Aspects.*

It is of the utmost importance that the international aspects of the industrial question should be constantly remembered. Industrial and social conditions in different parts of Africa and the East, including the exploitation of coloured labour and the labour of children, deliver a clear challenge to our Christian civilization. We are aware that difficult questions are involved : we may take South Africa as an illustration of the intricacy of the problem.

As regards South Africa, the Committee recognizes the complexity of the problem where the most highly skilled European labour is found side by side with a great mass of coloured, native, and Indian labour ranging from skilled to the roughest degree of unskilled capacity. It further acknowledges that in the development of a new country, with people whose wants are few and whose way of life is primitive, a lower rate of pay is for a time legitimate than would be reasonable or possible for civilized workers. But we consider that there are two dangers to be avoided. On the one hand there is the temptation to employers to reduce wages towards a level which would be acceptable to the less developed race, but insufficient and unfair to the more civilized On the other hand there is the greater danger of deliberate effort on the part of white men to check that advance of the natives and coloured people which missionary enterprise, education, and contact with civilization are gradually producing , and to exclude them by artificial barriers from a share in skilled employments. A mere " colour-bar " is, in our opinion, both economically and politically unsound, and religiously and morally indefensible. The Cape Province policy of " equal right for all civilized men " is the one which we hope to see extended throughout South Africa, and we welcome the recent repudiation by the Prime Minister, General Smuts, of any intention unjustly to exploit the native races.

The main issue is clear. First of all, we are bound to bring the principles of the Gospel to bear on inhuman and oppressive conditions of labour, whether they obtain at home or in the remote regions of the earth: secondly, we have to act upon the knowledge that the whole world is one and that the establishment of proper conditions of labour anywhere can only be secured on an international basis. We therefore cordially welcome the provisions of the Treaty of Peace which relate to labour, and the conventions and recommendations adopted by the International Labour Conference of the League of Nations at its first annual meeting. It is to be hoped that the process of international agreement thus begun may be carried to a complete fulfilment.

3. *Women in Industry.*

An important feature in the world of labour is the steady increase in the number of women engaged in industry. During the war, especially in the later years, the increase was very large, but that it was not merely temporary is shewn by the fact that there are still in England about three-quarters of a million more women in industry than in 1914.

In the future the numbers will probably tend still further to increase (allowing for fluctuations in trade) from the following causes :—

1. The newly-acquired capacity of women for all kinds of work, together with the tendency to " standardize," so that any one individual has only to learn to do quite a small part of the whole.

2. The fact that many women have tasted the joy of taking their part in the nation's life of industry, with a new sense of comradeship and independence.

3. The increase in the need of additional labour through the extension of industry.

It is most important at the present moment for all to give their most careful study and thought to the very difficult problems which are now confronting women in industry in their natural and legitimate claim for fair remuneration, and in their desire to maintain the highest ideals of family life (which must always form some part of a woman's life). Speaking generally the Church ought to insist that for married women the primary work is the work of the home.

Put briefly the main problem is this :—

1. Should the whole old system of " protected " women's work be restored ? The difficulty of answering this question is illustrated by the fate of the clauses concerning " two shifts " in the Bill recently introduced into the House of Commons.

2. Should the aim be to have perfect equality of wages *and* of conditions of work with men ?

And with regard to the second question :—

Should there be complete fusion of men's and women's work ? Or should women aim at confining themselves to the specialization of such work as would utilize women's particular gifts ?

All women are puzzled over these problems, and at present they have no decided line of policy ; it is the duty of the Church, therefore, to give much time and thought and sympathy to them in their difficulties.

4. *The Drink Question.*

Christian people will not be slow to recognize that moral evils lie at the root of our social disorders. If the devils of greed and selfishness were cast out, the battle would soon be won. There are also three specific evils which cause infinite harm to society—sexual impurity, gambling and intemperance. Sexual impurity, the most disastrous of the three, is dealt with by another Committee. On gambling we have nothing new to say. The evil is always with us, and we can only reiterate that the desire to get something for nothing, and the passion for excitement which it nourishes, are always demoralizing, and in their worst forms lead to utter corruption of character. The whole instinct of gambling is selfish and anti-social. The third evil, owing to recent developments, calls for more special treatment.

That an enormous amount of loss in efficiency in the industrial world, and of injury and suffering in our social life, is caused by drink is proved by an overwhelming amount of evidence. To this we earnestly call attention. Immediate and adequate action is required.

F

In the Report of the Lambeth Conference of 1888 on Intemperance (which was signed by Archbishop Temple) it is asserted that " if the whole Church had been thoroughly alive to the extent and nature of the mischief, much might have been done by more earnest efforts both of the Clergy and Laity in the ordinary course of the Church's work." These words may emphatically be repeated to-day.

In some directions much has been done. The Republic of the United States, after having tried prohibition for years in several individual states, has finally adopted the policy throughout its entire area Representatives from the United States offer ample evidence that this policy has already resulted in a marked decrease in the population of penal and charitable institutions, in the number of cases coming before the police and criminal courts, and in the demand upon rescue work. There is also an improvement in economic and industrial conditions, and above all in the stability of the home, the integrity of the family, and the welfare of children. The question is being so seriously considered in the Dominion of Canada that, with the exception of Quebec, all the provinces are at present under prohibitory law.

In New Zealand, Dominion prohibition was lost at a recent poll by a small majority. There is a strong feeling in that country that the elimination of the drink traffic would contribute to the efficiency and morality of the Dominion. It is a significant fact that no area in which prohibition has been carried on the three-fifths majority basis has gone back from its previous decision

In respect to the native races, we urge that the policy of prohibiting the importation of liquor should be strongly enforced, and that all social customs leading to the formation or increase of the drink habit amongst the natives be condemned as being especially dangerous to them. The trade in liquor with these defenceless people is one of the most disastrous instances of the exploiting of the weaker for the financial benefit of the stronger.

We earnestly hope that paragraph 5, Article XXII., of the Covenant of the League of Nations referring "to the prohibition of abuses such as the slave trade, the arms traffic, and the liquor traffic," will be expanded into definite provisions and speedily put into operation both as regards mandatory and general areas.

In regard to the United Kingdom, the Committee contents itself with a quotation from the Report of the Royal Commission on the Licensing Laws :—

" It is undeniable that a gigantic evil remains to be remedied, and hardly any sacrifice would be too great which would result in a marked diminution of this national degradation "

That no adequate sacrifice has yet been made is evidenced by the fact that last year £386,600,000 was spent in the United

Kingdom on strong drink. Under the restrictions imposed by the Board of Control during the war, the situation greatly improved. Since these have been in part removed, there has been a distinct relapse.

In the United Kingdom one of the chief hindrances to progress is the inability of those who are most earnest in promoting temperance reform to come to an agreement as to the best line of advance. All the English bishops on this committee are agreed on the desirability, for the United Kingdom, of fuller State control, of local option, and of the reform of public-houses: as regards State-purchase and prohibition there is difference of opinion among them.

In conclusion, we desire, with all the strength and earnestness which we possess, to urge upon our fellow Churchmen in every part of the world the imperative importance of giving the gravest consideration to the entire question of intemperance. We would add further that, whilst all are not agreed upon the duty of total abstinence from intoxicating liquor as a beverage, there is no room for doubt that such abstinence for the sake of others, and as a contribution to the stability of our industrial and social life, is a splendid privilege of Christian service.

III.

Our Primary Duty.

The primary duty of the Church (by which we mean the whole society of Christian men) is to witness to the principles of Christ and His Kingdom. The work of this Committee in setting forth those principles is greatly lightened by the recent publication of the Report of the Archbishops' Committee on Christianity and Industrial Problems (S.P.C.K. 1918). With the opinions and suggestions of that Report this Committee finds itself substantially in agreement They would, however, desire to emphasize the fact that while individual members of, or special groups within, the Church may rightly advocate some specific programme or policy, the Church should never, as a Body, concern itself with a political issue unless it involves a clear moral issue, and then only in the interest of morals and righteousness, and not in the interest of parties. On many industrial questions there is need for frank co-operation with the economist, and it is hardly necessary to state that, if material wealth is regarded not as an end but as a means, we must submit ourselves to scientific investigation of the processes that govern the production of wealth and the methods which guide us in its distribution. But we cannot accept the theory, which indeed is repudiated by modern economists, that man is to be regarded as a merely acquisitive animal. We desire to re-affirm the finding of the 1897 Committee : " Christian opinion ought to condemn the belief that economic conditions are to be left to the action of material causes and mechanical laws, uncontrolled by any moral responsibility." There is indeed a constant need for students of economy who will investigate these problems scientifically from a Christian standpoint. It will frequently be found that scientific economics require reinforcement by Christian ethics.

Two illustrations may be given.

(1) The great economic need of the present time is more production. It is for the economist to shew the disastrous fallacy of limitation of output. But the workman needs to be assured first that the right things are produced—things which contribute to beauty or to use, not superfluous futilities—and secondly, that the wealth which is produced will be justly distributed and devoted to the public good. If the workman is asked to sacrifice the interests of his class to the interests of the whole community, he needs to be convinced that the whole community is really going to reap the benefit of his labour. It is clear that bare economics will not take us to the goal. Mr. Hoover was right when he said that something like a spiritual revival is required if the industrial problem of production is to be solved.

(2) There is no economic question more important than that of the nature and function of capital. But it is an unreal abstraction which treats capital as possessing laws and movements of its own apart from the people who control it. For the use of capital, persons are responsible, and, if they are Christians, they cannot be satisfied with mere consideration of security and profit So long as the materialistic point of view is paramount, class war is inevitable If there is to be industrial peace we need the outlook and the motive which are supplied by our Christian Faith.

We turn then to those great principles which represent the Christian law of righteousness and love.

(1) *Human Value.*—As God is our Father, and as the Eternal Son of God took our whole human nature upon Him, every son and daughter of God is of infinite and equal value. There are wide differences in capacity, but such differences do not warrant any loss of liberty or any failure to give to all the children of God the opportunity of a full human life. Life must always count for more than property, the possession of which ought always to answer to some function duly performed. Therefore we are bound to condemn any system which regards men or women as mere instruments for the production of wealth. Obviously in any organized system there must be discipline : but that discipline should be the discipline of free men, arising from the common mind, and embodying the common will. If a man is

always expressing the ideals of others, with never a chance to express his own, his personality is denied its full development. Whether or no the demand for the full " democratizing of industry " is practicable or even reasonable, it is at least clear that the workers in an industry ought to have an adequate share in the control of the conditions under which their work—a large portion of their life—is carried on.

As a means of attaining this reasonable control, perfect freedom of organization on the part of workers, with leaders and spokesmen of their own choosing, must be upheld. Although this principle is accepted in England as an accomplished fact, it is evident that in some countries represented in this Conference there is need to bear witness to its reasonableness. If Trade-Unionism is liable to abuse—a danger which inheres in the exercise of all new-found power—it involves a valuable process of education. We invoke the principle of mutual respect, and the God-given grace of good-will, for managers of industry and likewise for the army of workers, that their separate organizations, through the willingness to look not only on their own things, but also on the things of others, may in God's time and in His own way be transcended in a larger fellowship.

This principle of human value also has a direct bearing on the vast subject of education. Our boys and girls should be trained not merely to be efficient producers of wealth, but to be their true selves, completely developed in body, mind, and spirit, so that they may give their full service to God and their fellows. Seeing that such education needs a lifetime for its fulfilment, we must warmly welcome every plan for its continuance, and aim not merely at a " ladder " for a few fortunate boys and girls, but at a highway which will open the best education in the country to all who are capable of profiting by it. With regard to adult education, such efforts as those of the Workers' Educational Association deserve the most earnest support.

Among the manifold tasks which this Conference has taken in hand it has been found impossible to include any special report on the subject of religious education—a subject which was dealt with very fully at the last Conference. All the more, therefore, do we feel constrained, in any treatment of the social duty of the Church, to insist that it must refuse to rest content until genuine religious teaching is recognized as a vital part of education.

(2) The principle of human value, with its insistence on the worth of the individual, needs for its complement the principle of *human brotherhood*, which teaches us that we are members one of another. The Incarnation broke down the ancient barriers. Differences of race, of class, of sex, are transcended : " we are one man in Christ Jesus."

The corollary of this principle of brotherhood, in relation to our industrial system, is that we must regard industry, not chiefly as a means of private profit or class advantage, but as an opportunity of service " for the glory of God and the good of man's estate." To quote Mr. W. L. Hichens : " Unless industry is really recognized as primarily a national service, in which each individual is fulfilling his function to the best of his ability for the sake of the community, in which private gain is subordinated to public good, in which, in a word, we carry out our duty towards our neighbour—unless we build on this foundation, there is no hope of creating the House Beautiful. If each man thinks of making his pile by all the means that economic individualism allows, if class bands itself against class, trade union against employers' federation, firm against firm, to secure the greatest share of the world's goods in unrestricted competition, social life must inevitably break down and anarchy reign supreme "

Now, so long as the present wage system lasts, there are certain lines of reform which, by almost universal confession, ought to be followed.

(a) *Security against Unemployment.*

It is beyond our compass to discuss methods of solving this troublesome problem. The difficulties are notoriously great, but it is certain that nothing is more fruitful of unrest than a haunting sense of insecurity in the mind of the workers : it cannot be right that a workman should be regarded as a mere tool to be scrapped when not required for another's use, and it is an offence to the conscience of a Christian community that men who are able and willing to work should be forced into idleness.

(b) *Reasonable Leisure.*

The constant subdivision of labour and the increasing use of machinery are an inevitable cause of wearisome monotony in the labour of many industrial workers. " The idea of the leisured classes and the toiling masses is monstrous : it is just the toiling drudge who needs leisure most—leisure for recreation and refreshment, leisure for education—above all, leisure for education." *

In some countries, however, where there is a large increase in the amount of leisure enjoyed by the worker, there is need of real help in ensuring that such leisure may be used for the happiness and good of all concerned, and such help may well be offered by the Church.

(c) *A Living Wage.*

We reaffirm the principle commended in an appendix to the 1908 Report. " The Christian Church, which holds that the

* Mr. W. L. Hichens, " Some Problems of Modern Industry."

individual life is sacred, must teach that it is intolerable to it that any part of our industry should be organised upon the foundation of the misery and want of the labourer   The fundamental Christian principle of the remuneration of labour is that the first charge upon any industry must be the proper maintenance of the labourer—an idea which it has been sought to express in popular language by the phrase ' the living wage.' "

This must not be interpreted as a bare subsistence wage. There must be sufficient to live a decent and complete, a cleanly and noble life.

(d) *Safeguards to Life and Health.*

" The Church should also urge upon its members the moral, as distinct from the legal, obligation of providing and making efficient whatever in the way of apparatus or arrangements is necessary to safeguard the life and health of the worker."

But there is a further question which has to be faced. While it is our immediate duty to remove, so far as may be, everything in the existing system which is an offence against liberty and brotherhood, we are also forced to ask whether the present system is compatible with the law of Christ. Bishop Westcott said quite plainly : " Wage labour, though it appears to be an inevitable step in the evolution of society, is as little fitted to represent finally or adequately the connection of man with man in the production of wealth as, in earlier times, slavery or serfdom." Two characteristics of the order to which the wage system belongs are the pursuit of self-interest and the prevalence of unrestricted competition. Now self-interest has a legitimate, though always a subordinate, place in Christian ethics ; and competition, not for mere gain but for the fulfilment of duty in the best possible way, is a reasonable incentive to efficiency. It is foolish to despise individual enterprise and unduly to fetter individual liberty. But the dominant principle in a rightly ordered society will be co-operation for the common good rather than competition for private advantage. It cannot be said that this principle rules our present system. No doubt it will be urged that if the motives which support the present order are removed, the whole industrial system is in danger of collapsing. But as Christians we cannot accept the assumption that men will only be induced to work by the incentive of large gain or by the stimulus of imminent personal want. It was a higher motive that led men and women to offer their devoted service, often at the cost of sacrificing life itself, during the years of war. Is it wholly incredible that such motives may be forthcoming in time of peace ?

It certainly would seem that the principle laid down by Dr. Headlam (in the course of a trenchant criticism of the Report of the Archbishops' Committee on " Christianity and Industrial Problems "), " the substitution of a strong spirit of brotherhood for a spirit of competition or rivalry," must lead us to a profound dissatisfaction with the existing order ; nor do we dispute his warning " to meddle as little as possible, as a Church, with definite political or economic issues," if it is rightly interpreted.

It is, in fact, not our business to pronounce on the respective merits of rival methods for creating a better order, *e.g.*, " Nationalization," or " Guild Socialism," or " Labour co-partnership." Nor again do we for a moment utter any general condemnation of the captains of industry who have had the main responsibility for working our present system. It is superfluous to say that many of them have been and are men of the highest integrity and honour, whose chief motive has not been mere pursuit of gain, but who have sought to render good service to the community, and, in rendering it, to exercise the most scrupulous care for the welfare of the employees.

But we repeat that co-operation for the common good is the goal towards which the industrial journey of society should be directed. That goal can never be reached by violent revolution. Mr Bertrand Russell (himself not adverse to communism) has written: " The damage to civilization done by revolution in one country may be repaid by the influence of another, in which there has been no revolution, but in a universal cataclysm civilization might go under for 1,000 years."

Perhaps we shall not be transgressing our limitations if we suggest that the next line of advance towards the expression of brotherhood in industry is to be found in those industrial parliaments, where employers and employed meet on absolutely equal terms, of which the English building trade affords a notable example. The condition of their success is open confidence, frank goodwill, and the determination, on both sides, to keep all promises and fulfil all undertakings.

(3) From the principle of human brotherhood we pass to that of *human responsibility*. God trusts us. We are responsible for the right use of our capacities and endowments, and we are responsible for one another. All that belongs to us is held in trust : no property can be our absolute and unconditional possession. This is true also of our powers and faculties of body and mind. These powers are entrusted to us by God in order that we may use them for His service and the good of our fellows : the duty of honest work, to the uttermost of our ability, is binding upon all, and we cannot, without moral deterioration, rest content with less than our best work. The idler or the shirker, to whatever class of society he belongs, is false to his trust. It is true that a labourer is worthy of his hire ; it is equally true that the worker ought to do an honest day's work : the

policy of ' ca' canny ' or ' go slow ' cannot be morally justified : on the other hand, those whose work is " unproductive " of material wealth are specially bound to give good value to society in return for the benefits which society confers on them.

The principle of responsibility covers our relation to each other. A man is his " brother's keeper "; the public is responsible for industrial conditions, and the selfishness of the consumer is at least as pronounced as the selfishness of the producer ; moreover, in our complex civilization, the whole community is responsible for the conditions under which any section of it is compelled to live. It is true enough that in the abnormal conditions of our time problems like that of housing may baffle even the most resolute efforts. But it is a reproach to our Christian civilization that we have tolerated, both in town and country, slums and unsanitary dwellings which have caused an appalling mortality among little children, and have been plague spots of disease and moral evil. " Overcrowding," said Sir Charles Booth, " is the most fruitful cause of drunkenness and vice." Even where the worst features of the slum have been absent, we have allowed our industrial towns to become a mean wilderness of hideous streets. Almost everywhere the miserably inadequate supply of houses leads to the gravest moral difficulty and danger. The way of remedy is hard to find, but our conscience cannot be easy until we have found it.

Before we pass to the suggestion of various lines of action in the Church to-day, we may briefly sum up the position at which we have arrived.

Because God is our Father, all His children are of infinite value. To each of His children should be given the best possible opportunity of a full human life : life must count for more than property, and no human being ought ever to be used for less than a human purpose.

Because all men are brothers of Jesus Christ, all artificial barriers must be broken down. Where there is true brotherhood men will work together in service for the common good : they will cease to strive one against another for mere private advantage.

Because God trusts us, we are responsible for all that we possess, and we are responsible for the care of each other. " If one member suffer, all the members suffer with it." The reform of evil conditions—such as bad housing—is the business of the whole body.

The fulfilment of these principles must lead to something better than a " tinkering scheme of piecemeal reform " Yet it is not by violent revolution, but by a complete change of mind and will that a better order can be reached. So far as the immediate future is concerned, it is possible to take steps without delay to meet the evils of unemployment, and to secure for all workers a living wage, reasonable leisure, and a share in the control of the conditions in which their working life is spent.

IV.

How to Fulfil our Duty.

(1) The bare statement of these principles shews us the truth in Mr. Chesterton's dictum, " Christianity has been found difficult and has not been tried." Most of us have grave cause for repentance. We have failed to give faithful witness in our teaching : we have failed even more signally to give witness *by our life*. Here, surely, is our first duty. It was the life of the early Christians which won victories for Christ. It is the life of Christians which will do most to further His Kingdom in the society of to-day. Members of the Christian Church must repudiate the standards of the world. They must " take heed and beware of covetousness." It ought not to be possible to say that many of them are as unscrupulous as any pagan in exploiting their own economic advantage. A Christian will repudiate the maxim that " business is business "—the equivalent in industry of the Prussian maxim, " war is war." His sense of honour will be as keen in his commercial dealings as in his personal intercourse : he will think about his duties before he thinks about his rights : he will be courteous, considerate, and kindly towards all, whether they are supposed to belong to a " higher " or " lower" grade in society : he will be scrupulously careful about the nature of his investments, and will avoid expenditure which merely tends to vulgar display or selfish indulgence : he will honour a man, not for his success in making money, but for his service to the common good : his ambition for himself and his children will be the contribution of useful service to the community, not the attainment of wealth or social position. The witness of his life will, in a word, be the witness of one who tries to follow the Christian law of love.

(2) The witness of the individual will be reinforced if the whole Church is, what it ought to be, a warm-hearted brotherly fellowship. In the New Testament " philadelphia," love for members of the Christian community, was the necessary precursor of " agape," love of all men for Christ's sake. It was not in irony that the heathen said, " see how these Christians love one another." In the early Church it was recognized that a brother must be helped to find employment. If he was unable to work he was provided with support. If he would not work " neither should he eat." Class distinctions were no barrier : the man of noble birth believed in and acted on his brotherhood with the despised slave at whose side he had received his communion.

No one can pretend that this is true of the Church to-day. Class consciousness is rampant in every grade of society. In many of our churches the arrangement of "sittings" would incur the condemnation of St. James Can we not determine to get rid once for all of unbrotherly aloofness, and to abolish the mis-interpretation of the Church Catechism which represents "my betters" as meaning "social superiors"

There are signs of improvement. For example, men and women of all classes are taking their places in our various Church Councils. But we need to make careful provision to open the door wide for representatives of the industrial class

We may be thankful, also, that we are well on the road to carry out some recommendations of the "Moral Witness" Committee of the 1908 Conference :—

> "It is of the greatest importance, therefore . . . that the Church of Christ, if it is to win the confidence of the democracy, should show its readiness to set its own house in order ; to model its own system of government on a sound, representative, and democratic basis ; to restore the ministry of the laity to its legitimate place and power in Church government and discipline ; to exhibit such business capabilities in the administration of Church finance as shall at least provide adequate stipends and pensions for its clergy, reapportion and readjust where necessary existing resources for this purpose, furnish sufficient funds for the upkeep of Church fabrics and for the organisation of the charitable and philanthropic institutions of the Church ; and, above all, to make impossible the abuses too often connected with Church patronage."

It may be added that we ought to do our utmost to further the efforts already made to enable men of all classes, whose vocation and capacity are proved, to receive the necessary training for the Ministry of the Church. Experience in connection with Service Candidates is full of encouragement.

(3) Another recommendation of previous Conferences has been only partially followed, viz., *Association within the Anglican Communion for study and for practical social work*. It is greatly to be desired that a Social Service Committee should be established in each diocese, with branches, if possible, in every congregation, and other parts of the Church might well follow the example of Canada and the U S A by forming a Council which should act for the whole Church and watch for special social needs and opportunities. As regards England, reference may here be made to the work of the Christian Social Union and the Industrial Christian Fellowship, which have now been fused into one society, the purpose of which is to further the Kingdom of God in social and industrial life, and, in its presentation of the Gospel message to those engaged in industry, to shew the full application of Christianity to social life and practice.

(4) But there is need for *wider association with other Christians in social witness and service*. It belongs to another Committee

to deal with the anxious problems of reunion among Christians ; but, whatever be the delays in the restoration of communion upon doctrinal and sacramental grounds, we believe that there are no principles at stake which can rightly be held to hinder all denominations of Christians from beginning without any delay to act as if they were wholly one body in the department of public, moral, and social witness. We dare, further, to affirm that nothing serves better to promote the deeper sort of union than the mutual knowledge engendered by working closely together in social service ; and also that, short of the witness of full sacramental union, there can be no more impressive witness for Christianity than the spectacle of a Christendom re-united so far as to be able to stand together for the application of the principles of justice and brotherhood in society and industry. We ought to add that we are thinking not only or chiefly of Central Committees, of conspicuous religious leaders in great capital cities, but local councils gathering in each centre of population the representatives of all the Christian congregations of the locality. Already considerable progress has been made in many towns of the British Empire and the U.S.A. Civic guilds or social service councils or community centres have been formed for the purpose of detecting abuses which need reform, of focusing a sound public opinion, of supporting the municipal authorities in the pursuit not of sectional interests, but of the common good, and of furthering every kind of useful social work. The Christian Social Crusade in England, and corresponding organizations in other countries, have done much to promote this purpose. In many cases the inter-denominational guild has formed close alliances with Labour and other movements, which aim at a better social order.

(5) The Church should be a *reservoir of social service.* There is a large and almost infinitely varied field of service both for men and women who will find the vocation of their life in social ministry, and for those who are able only to devote their leisure to it. Welfare work of all kinds, after-care committees for school-children, club work, study circles, and other efforts to promote fellowship and utilize leisure—these are only specimens of an enormous choice of opportunities.* Special reference may here be made to the work of the Church Army for lifting up those who are down. While there is great need of men and

---

* It is hardly necessary to add that any form of social service deserves to be taken seriously with a full sense of its responsibility, and careful training is required. We would urge that in any scheme of training in economics, theology should find a place, in order that its true motive-power for the work may be given. Most of the Universities have now agreed to accept Theology as one of their optional subjects.

Very useful suggestions are given in " The Church and Social Service," Report of the Archbishop of Canterbury's Committee (S.P.C K , 1920).

women who will give themselves to the distinctively pastoral 'and evangelistic lay ministry of the Church, it should be emphasized that all work of social welfare, undertaken from the right motive and in the right spirit, is "Church work." The Recruiting Campaign for Service in the Kingdom of God has laid stress on the close connection between Missionary and Social Service It is earnestly to be hoped that the splendid devotion shewn by countless men and women during the war may find a new and even greater opportunity, in working along different but converging roads towards the establishment of righteousness, fellowship, and love between the nations and within the nations of the world.

V.

THE ROOT OF THE MATTER.

We have suggested various lines of action which, we feel assured, it is our duty to follow, if we are to arrive at that better social and industrial order which we believe to be in accordance with God's will But we desire to affirm, with unwavering conviction, that no outward adjustments can, by themselves, bring us near to the Kingdom of God. The love which conquers selfishness, and the passion for righteousness which drives out greed, are gifts from above, and, unless selfishness and greed are vanquished, the most perfectly devised co-operative commonwealth will perish in ignoble ruin. There is doubtless a narrow other-worldliness which seeks a selfish security in another life, but the principles and powers of the other world offer the only hope of redemption for the individual and for society. Man has an eternal destiny, and his whole nature is therefore of infinite worth. To uplift humanity, and to redeem every child of man, the Son of God came into this world. By His Incarnation He gave us the complete revelation of human duty. By His Cross and Passion He taught us the true value of life and death, and opened that way of fellowship with God, without which there can be no real fellowship of man with man. By the power of His Resurrection and the living inspiration of His Spirit, the ultimate victory will be won : and the Church which is His Body can go forward, with confident hope, to fulfil by prayer and work and witness its Mission of seeking that Kingdom of love and righteousness which He will one day reveal in its perfect beauty.

(Signed) J. A LICHFIELD,

Chairman

No. III.

REPORT OF THE COMMITTEE† APPOINTED TO CONSIDER AND REPORT UPON THE SUBJECT OF THE DEVELOPMENT OF PROVINCES IN THE ANGLICAN COMMUNION.

"IF the Anglican Communion is to render that service to the varied needs of mankind to which the Church of our day is specially called, regard must be had both to the just freedom of its several parts, and to the just claims of the whole Communion upon its every part." It is in the spirit of these words, quoted from the Encyclical Letter of the Lambeth Conference of 1908, that your Committee on the "Development of Provinces in the Anglican Communion" has tried to act, and to make some suggestions. It recognizes the fact that in the Lambeth Conference of 1867 the system of provincial organization was primarily laid down. It recognizes, too, that on the principles of the system then laid down such organization has been carried out in various parts of the world. It feels consequently that its special work this year is to deal with the development of that system, in the Church as it exists to-day, with the view of making that organization more complete and effective.

† Names of Members of the Committee :—

Bishop of Accra
Bishop of Ballarat*
Bishop Hamilton Baynes (*Secretary*)
Bishop of Brechin (Primus)*
Archbishop of Brisbane
Bishop of Bunbury
Archbishop of Capetown (*Chairman*)
Bishop of Chekiang
Bishop of Christchurch
Bishop of Colombo
Bishop of George
Bishop of Gibraltar
Bishop of Goulburn
Bishop of Grantham
Bishop of Honduras
Bishop of Jamaica
Bishop of Kalgoorlie
Bishop of Lagos
Bishop of Manchester

Bishop of Massachusetts
Archbishop of Melbourne*
Bishop of Newfoundland
Bishop of New Jersey
Bishop in North China
Bishop of Northern Rhodesia
Archbishop of Nova Scotia
Bishop of Ohio
Bishop of Oklahoma
Bishop of Osaka
Bishop Osborne
Bishop of Richmond
Bishop of Rochester
Archbishop of Rupert's Land
Bishop of St Helena
Bishop in Shantung
Bishop of Uganda*
Archbishop of the West Indies
Bishop of Worcester
Bishop of Zanzibar

In the first place your Committee has learnt that a considerable number of Dioceses, now amounting to 31, have been established in many parts of the world, which are not as yet included in any sort of provincial organization of their own.[*]

This is a sign of growth for which there is cause for much thankfulness : but at the same time it is evident that if these Dioceses were grouped into provincial organizations such grouping would tend to the health and strength not only of those Dioceses immediately concerned but of the Church in general.

Your Committee therefore suggests that whenever and wherever it may be possible, new Provinces be created, and that Dioceses now working in isolation be encouraged to attach themselves to some existing Province or to form a new Province. Your Committee is aware that many of these Dioceses are of a purely missionary character, and consequently it seems necessary to point out that the one organization which is essential to provincial life is a House or College of Bishops. Your Committee suggests that it is advisable in any newly-constituted Provincial Synod for the Bishops to associate with themselves the Clergy and Laity of the Province as soon as may be. When, however, local circumstances make such association impracticable, this need be no hindrance to the initiation of a provincial organization.

In such cases each National or Regional Church or Province would necessarily determine its own constitutional and canonical enactments. Its Bishops would take an oath of Canonical obedience to the new Metropolitan of the Province or of conformity to such other Authority as may be constitutionally appointed. This would refer to all Bishops, both those already working in the newly-constituted Province and those who shall be thereafter consecrated for work in any See within the provincial area. In order to comply with the Canonical rule for the consecration of a Bishop within the Province, your Committee suggests that in the formation of a new Province a minimum of four Dioceses shall be required.

Questions relating to the appointment of Bishops must be left to the newly-constituted Province to decide, but the Committee suggests that in the election of a Metropolitan, the Province as well as the Diocese should have a real and distinct voice.

In respect to problems of race and language, which have been brought before it, the Committee feels that these are

[*] Your Committee is glad to learn that there would seem to be an immediate prospect of the branches of our Communion in China and Japan obtaining full advantage of any rights attaching to provincial organization, and further of the possible formation of new Provinces among the Dioceses of East and West Africa.

matters which must be left to the various Provinces or Regional Churches to settle, but it would lay down one distinct principle, namely, that in every Province there can be but one Church and one Authority.

Your Committee is of opinion that the position of the Consultative Body of the Lambeth Conference should be strengthened. It consequently expresses the hope, first, that all parts of the Anglican Communion may see their way to nominate representatives on that Body, so that it may be representative of the whole Church ; secondly, that this Consultative Body may be increasingly regarded as a real living Body, to which any question of Faith and Order may be referred, as an authority of great moral weight, providing a voluntary nexus for the whole of the Anglican Communion though possessing no power to enforce its decisions. That this was the intention of the establishment of the Consultative Body there cannot be a doubt, and your Committee feels that it may help towards this end if its constitution and functions are reasserted at this Conference.

It also suggests that while the manner of appointment of members of this Body must be left to the various Provinces or Churches, members should be appointed for a period of not more than five years.

As one question of wide concern which the Consultative Body might profitably consider the Committee suggests the Colonial Clergy Act and its possible modification.

NOTE.—In the foregoing Report the Conference has had chiefly in view the formation of Provinces by the synthesis of isolated Dioceses, not by the sub-division of National Churches as in the United States of America.

(Signed) WILLIAM M. CAPETOWN,
Chairman.

No. IV.

REPORT OF THE COMMITTEE † APPOINTED TO CONSIDER AND REPORT UPON "MISSIONARY PROBLEMS": (a) MISSIONS AND GOVERNMENTS, (b) MISSIONS AND GROWING CHURCHES; (c) LITURGICAL VARIATIONS; (d) MARRIAGE QUESTIONS

THE MISSIONARY CALL.

OUR Blessed Lord has made it the duty of every one of His people no less than of the Church at large or her leaders, to see that His Kingdom is extended by making disciples of all nations, and established by training them in His laws. The building up in holiness of existing congregations, and the winning of new ones, are two parts of one task, never to be separated. Each is necessary to the other. The older Church must be purified and quickened, if it is to be capable of its evangelistic function;

† Names of Members of the Committee :—

Bishop of Antigua.
Bishop of Athabasca.
Bishop of Auckland.
Bishop of Bendigo.
Bishop of Buckingham.
Bishop of Calcutta (*Chairman*)
Archbishop of Capetown
Bishop of Carpentaria.
Bishop of Chekiang.
Bishop of Clogher.
Bishop Copleston
Bishop in Corea.
Bishop of Dornakal.
Bishop of Exeter
Bishop of Falkland Isles.
Bishop of Fukien.
Bishop of Gippsland.
Bishop of Grantham.
Bishop of Hankow.
Bishop of Honan
Bishop of Honduras
Bishop Ingham
Bishop of Kimberley.
Bishop King
Bishop of Kwangsi.
Bishop of Lagos.

Bishop of Long Island.
Bishop of Mackenzie River.
Bishop of Moosonee
Bishop of Newark.
Bishop of New Guinea.
Bishop of New Mexico
Bishop in North China
Bishop of North Queensland.
Bishop of Northern Rhodesia.
Bishop of North Texas.
Bishop of Nyasaland (*Secretary*)
Bishop Oluwole.
Bishop in Persia.
Bishop Price.
Bishop Roach (Natal Assistant Bishop)
Bishop of St John's.
Bishop of Saskatchewan.
Bishop of Singapore.
Bishop of Southern Rhodesia.
Bishop in South Tokyo.
Bishop in Tinnevelly.
Bishop of Tokyo.
Bishop of Western China.
Bishop of West Missouri.
Bishop of Zululand

and the exercise of that function is a condition of its health. It is always found that the Church or the Parish in which the missionary spirit is most active is the most abundantly enriched with all spiritual blessings There is no question here of a Home Department and a Foreign Department. This is not a counsel of perfection. It is implicit in discipleship itself; it cannot rightly be evaded.

Yet we confess with shame that the prayers and efforts which belong to the missionary spirit still fall far short—in spite of real and increasing improvement—of what loyalty and love to Christ demand. Bishops and Parish Priests must preach this duty more constantly · the public prayers must be full of it : in every council of the Church, from the Parish to the General Synod, it must hold a conspicuous place among the Agenda : it must be among the cherished aims of every Christian home, of every Christian heart. For it is unreasonable that men should claim a place in the fellowship of the Church unless they are ready to share this obligation, which the Lord laid upon all disciples, at all times, in all places, amid all ordinary occupations as well as by direct evangelization, to be witnesses for Him

The aim that all His members must set before themselves may be quite simply stated thus : World-wide witness to the Lord. This does not necessarily mean immediate world conversion ; but it does mean adding to the Church daily such as are being saved. We aim immediately at the planting of Church life and order in all lands, at the formation of Churches, not only the conversion of individuals ; Churches which from the very first shall be active centres of evangelization ; at extending not the Anglican Church with its special characteristics, but the Holy Catholic Church in its essentials, which each new Church, as it grows up, may exhibit under characteristics of its own. Ultimately, we aim at all that is hoped for in the coming of the Kingdom of God.

HOME ORGANIZATION.

We enquire then what are the methods actually in use, in our dioceses and congregations, to rally all hearts to prayer and self-sacrifice, to kindle in the whole Body this missionary temper, and to secure its fullest expression and efficiency as a missionary force. We find, to speak generally, two distinct, but not quite incompatible, methods : one, that which the newer Churches have almost universally adopted, as in itself the normal way, and arising out of the nature of the Church ; namely, the method by which the whole Body is so " organized for Missions," that one current of enthusiasm and activity flows through and out of every member, every group and every individual ; the other, that in which, as the gradual result of various circumstances in the older Churches, certain great chartered Societies, and other Associations of Churchmen, have acted as specialized channels, through which the energy of the Body has found itself flowing.

In the Churches which are organized for Missions (for instance, in the United States and in Canada), the whole Body is one missionary organ : great decisions are made in full Synod, and the immediate executive is in the hands of a Board or Committee, over which the Synod or Convention is ultimately supreme. In some cases the financial obligation is distributed by the central authority among dioceses and parishes, by a system of apportionment or assessment : this method of assessment, though it is not everywhere at first popular, is on the whole, we are told, effective. This organization for Missions, to which the large English-speaking Churches have come completely or in part, is being adopted spontaneously and, so to speak, instinctively by the indigenous Churches of other races ; in the dioceses, for instance, of Uganda, of Nigeria, of Dornakal ; in the Churches of our Communion in Japan and China (the Nippon Sei Kokwai and the Chung-hua Sheng Kung Hui). Sometimes the diocese, sometimes the Province, is the unit, but in all such cases the initiative and the control are synodical.

The system which we have called the normal method is probably admitted on all hands to be in itself the better ; but it is not to be expected, or even to be desired, that it should be suddenly adopted by all. Where the method of Society organiza- tion exists, we recommend that it should be used to the full. We believe that it can be used to the full within a Church which is itself, as a Church, conscious of its own corporate mission. Societies are already working in co-operation with Synods, or in subordination to them. A central Advisory Council may guide, or wisely influence, all the agencies by which zeal is aroused, funds collected, and workers recruited, and may direct their associated energies to the needs of the enterprises, which from time to time are seen to be most urgent or most hopeful.

In England, some such co-ordination of agencies has been aimed at—but on a small scale, and tentatively—by the Central Board of Missions. That Board exists in order to represent and express the mind of the Church in respect to its work over- seas. Its constitution is framed with the view of giving to Missions overseas their rightful place as a primary activity of the whole Church, and in its present form it was formally adopted by the Convocations of Canterbury and York and by the Houses of Laymen of both Provinces—these bodies themselves all meeting together in what was the Representative Church Council. The creation of the National Assembly of the Church of England with statutory powers, able to give expression to the voice of the Church on all matters which concern it, has produced a new condition. If the National Assembly is to fulfil its purpose, it must give an important place to that which is accepted as a primary activity of the Church, and must make itself responsible for expressing the mind of the Church in all that belongs to its overseas work With this in view, it is desirable that the Central Board of Missions should be brought under the control of the National Assembly, from which it should receive its authority, and that the National Assembly should give in its deliberations a definite place to the Report of the Board—a place at least equal in importance to that of the other matters with which it deals. The decisions, recommendations and appeals would go forth as those not of a Board but of the Church itself.

We urge that it is of the utmost importance that this task should be taken up by the National Assembly from its first inception ; that it should be assumed as one of its normal and most precious functions ; that the Assembly should claim, from the first, and as a whole, to be the supreme missionary authority, superseding none but embracing and co-ordinating all

Our limits do not allow us to deal with those essential parts of the Home Church's work, for the sake of which the organizations we have been treating of exist. Of financial methods and necessities, we can here say nothing. In reference to the supply of workers, we note with thankfulness what has been done or set going in English dioceses by " the Recruiting Campaign." Besides men and women already recruited and sent to dioceses overseas, a large number of the Clergy have been enrolled as recognizing the principle of the oneness of the Ministry whether overseas or at home, and as pledging themselves to give equal consideration to calls which may come to them from either part of the One Field.

The need of clergy is urgent in some Colonial Dioceses whose large districts are being rapidly peopled, and the Conference should earnestly appeal to men in Great Britain to volunteer for pioneer work as well as to the men of the Churches in those lands to give themselves to the service of God in their own country.

We cannot leave unmentioned the paramount importance of missionary Study ; and in particular we desire to emphasize the value of information collected and brought within the reach of all, concerning what each separate agency is doing or planning. Such information should include the work of missionaries of other communions than our own. Finally, we acknowledge— sure that such acknowledgements can never be mere platitudes —that the One Agent of all missionary operations is the Holy Spirit of God, and that the largest contribution any man or woman can make to this Cause is that which is made by loving, faithful and persevering Prayer, he who truly gives this will not long keep back anything that he has

MISSIONS AND GROWING CHURCHES.

In reviewing the development of Missions into indigenous self-governing Churches in non-Christian lands, we are confronted with so much diversity, that it is extremely difficult to generalize. Some Dioceses have from the first developed their organization on the lines recommended below ; others have of late years been taking steps in a similar direction.

At the outset we wish to place on record our appreciation of the work of Missionary Societies and Boards of Missions. Their great progress has made their aim of establishing self-governing, self-supporting, and self-extending Churches, and themselves withdrawing from control and pushing their work further afield, possible in many mission fields at the present time.

The Committee therefore makes the following suggestions as to the immediate steps which should be taken to achieve this object.

Development of Local Churches.

I. There is in many missions a tendency to make the work centre in the Mission organization rather than in the Church. We would therefore urge that from the very beginning, the Mission staff should develop the Church consciousness of their people by the creation of consultative and executive councils in parish and district : and further, that such councils should as soon as possible find their place in a definite Diocesan system.

It is moreover important that all missionary committees and councils should as soon as possible be thoroughly representative of the congregations whose affairs they administer, instead of being, as is sometimes the case, predominantly representative of the subscribers to the mission alone : and further that care should be taken to avoid over-centralization of authority, or over-refinement of rules and procedure, both of which have been shewn by experience to retard the development of the corporate life of local churches

II. The question of the management of the finances which the Missionary Societies supply to the local Church is one of some delicacy. The principle that the provision of funds by a Society at home carries with it an inherent right to full control in the Mission has now been largely abandoned. But on the other hand, the Missionary Societies and Boards not unnaturally claim that they cannot be deprived of all share in the regulation of the work to which they contribute. The exact adjustment of the two claims will vary according to the progress of the Church which receives help. But we desire to express our conviction that an increasing share in the management of finance will call forth increased gifts from the indigenous churches, and will do more than anything else to strengthen their sense of responsibility and power of self-government We therefore urge the Missionary Societies and Boards to review their organization with a view to developing as generous a financial policy as possible. And we confidently appeal to the indigenous churches to respond with self-sacrifice and zealous work, in the matter of the support of their own parishes as well as in the wider work of the Church.

III. The Committee cannot but view with concern the widespread reluctance of those who should be the natural leaders of the churches abroad, to find their life's work in the ministries of the Church From many mission lands we hear the testimony that the organization of Mission and Church is conceived on lines so foreign, and the opportunities for a life of such service as shall be the natural and full expression of national gifts are so limited, that the best men are fain to turn to other walks of life.

We feel that the fault too often lies in the system which cannot find a congenial sphere for such men. They are conscious of membership in the Body of Christ, but they find scant opportunity of bringing their best to the service of the Body

We would strongly urge that both Missions and Dioceses should do their utmost so to organize their work that the widest freedom may be given for the development of the national and individual gifts of all who are called to the service of God and of His Church

IV Among the many problems which arise in carrying out any large transference of the centre of authority from the Mission to the Diocese, one stands out as peculiarly difficult : the settlement of a Diocese in which Europeans and indigenous congregations exist side by side in one area. We are clear that Catholic principle traditionally demands the territorial bishopric. But in such cases we must recognize that the marked differences of ideal and discipline, language and mentality demand that provision should be made in the one Synod or Province for the utmost freedom of development of the races side by side. In view of possible difficulties which may arise in securing this freedom while never losing sight of the ideal of the one Catholic Church, the Committee would call attention to Resolutions 24 of 1897 and 22 of 1908. The solution in each case must be left with the Province, but, whatever interim measures be adopted, we are clear that the ideal of the one Church must never be abandoned.

Missionary Societies Still Indispensable

V. But when all has been said in favour of the transfer of responsibilities to the local Churches, the need of the work of missionary societies remains as urgent as ever. Large areas of the world are still unevangelized ; the British Empire and America are taking ever-increasing responsibilities for the care of the backward races, and this is no time for a relaxation of the missionary effort of the home Churches in the partially evangelized fields also, we may mention three departments where ever-increasing help from the Missionary Societies is indispensable.

(1) *Evangelistic work*, both in the districts where a large influx of new converts still requires the fostering care of the mission, and in the large outlying districts in which local Churches have not at present the means to undertake the work

(2) *Institutional work*, such as colleges, schools and hospitals These are too costly for the local Churches wholly to maintain, and in them the experience and devotion of the foreign missionary are urgently needed

(3) *Women's work* The Mission Churches owe more than can be adequately expressed to the devoted service of women missionaries, and it is essential that this help should be continued and extended Special circumstances in some Oriental lands make an early transfer of women's work to the indigenous Churches impossible, and the organization of the Missions must be maintained Their work should however be more closely related to the local Church organization, and women can at least by means of Diocesan boards and councils be given their due place in the control of their own work which has its peculiar problems.

LITURGICAL VARIATIONS.

Previous Lambeth Conferences have recognized* the need for the adaptation and enrichment of the services of the "Book of Common Prayer and Administration of the Sacraments and other Rites and Ceremonies of the Church according to the Use of the Church of England " to meet the needs and conditions of races and countries overseas. But with the development of self-consciousness in the indigenous Churches a widespread demand has arisen throughout the Mission Field not only for some adaptation and enrichment of the existing book of Common Prayer, but for forms and services constructed otherwise than those in that Book

The principle of uniformity expounded in the Preface to the English Prayer Book, (which Preface was not drawn up in the light of conditions such as now exist in the Mission Field,) is neither applicable to Dioceses and Provinces in the Mission Field, nor in itself necessary as a bond of union between Churches which have unity of faith.

* Resolutions viii (1867), 10 (1888), 45 (1897), 24 and 27 (1908).

The essential elements in liturgical forms are few and simple. But over and above these indispensable elements, there is much that is common to the authorized Prayer Books of our Communion which it is desirable and convenient to preserve in any service-books that may be independently constructed, both on grounds of intrinsic and general merit, and as serving to maintain continuity and to promote corporate feeling between the faithful in different parts of our Communion.

We therefore recommend that :—

(i) Rigid liturgical uniformity is not to be regarded as a necessity throughout the Churches of the Anglican Communion in the Mission Field.

(ii) It should be recognized that full liberty belongs to Diocesan Bishops not only for the adaptations and additions alluded to above but also for the adoption of other uses.

(iii) In the exercise of this liberty care should always be taken :—

(a) To maintain a Scriptural and Catholic balance of Truth.

(b) To give due consideration to the precedents of the early Church.

(c) To observe such limitations as may be imposed by higher synodical authority.

(d) To remember with brotherly consideration the possible effect their action may have on other Provinces and Branches of the Anglican Communion.

The preparation of forms of service, and especially of an Order for the celebration of the Holy Communion, calls for the highest liturgical skill and knowledge, such as is not always available in every Province, and we believe that the best interests of the Church will be served by the appointment of a permanent Committee of experts in liturgical studies to which, when engaged in such tasks, the various Dioceses and Provinces might turn for advice.

HOLY MATRIMONY.

To avoid confusion we state at once that we regard Christian marriage as the marriage of Christians ; that such a marriage can only be made by the mutual consent before witnesses of both parties to an exclusive, lifelong union ; that it is for local ecclesiastical authorities to state publicly what can be accepted as sufficient evidence of this consent ; that in ordinary circumstances in countries where the State has made laws on this subject (i e , on what constitutes such evidence), it is desirable that the Church should accept them when possible ; that while the presence or absence of the Church's blessing does not affect the validity of marriage it is the plain duty of all Christians to seek the blessing of the Church on their marriage

That the marriages of non-Christian persons, though not of necessity exclusive or lifelong, are states of life in which they can and do live without sin, and that where both parties to such a marriage become Christians, the marriage is raised by Baptism to the level of Christian marriage, and must be reckoned as exclusive and lifelong

With regard to marriages contracted by non-Christians, good in the non-Christian Law, but contrary to Christian Law, we re-affirm the resolution of the Lambeth Conference of 1888 :

RESOLUTION 5 —" *That it is the opinion of this Conference that persons living in polygamy be not admitted to baptism, but that they be accepted as candidates and kept under Christian instruction until such time as they shall be in a position to accept the law of Christ.*"

"*That the wives of polygamists may, in the opinion of this Conference, be admitted in some cases to baptism, but that it must be left to the local authorities to decide under what circumstances they may be baptised.*"

We are of opinion that if a polygamist wishes to separate from his wives and be baptized, care must be taken that he make proper arrangements for the separated wives before he can be accepted.

We suggest that where the local authorities decide against the baptism of such persons, they may well be associated in some form of guild provided for them, so as to keep them in touch with Christian life.

A person married as a non-Christian to a person whose relationship to him or her is within the degrees prohibited by the Christian Church, cannot be baptized so long as that partner lives, unless they separate after due arrangement made for the future of the wife

A marriage, although potentially polygamous, or potentially dissoluble, should be regarded as a good marriage, capable of becoming exclusive and lifelong, in virtue of the baptism of both parties to it, and *ipso facto* becoming so if the baptism takes place In such cases the parties should not be re-married after baptism, but it is desirable that the fact of the marriage should be publicly acknowledged, and the parties to it should receive the Church's marriage blessing before being admitted to Holy Communion It is not intended by this to imply that where one party only is baptized, that party should be excluded from Communion until both have been so, but that after the baptism of the second, they should receive the blessing on their marriage, now fully Christian, and then as Christian man and wife receive Holy Communion together.

A marriage potentially polygamous or potentially dissoluble is not raised to the level of Christian marriage by the baptism of one party If after such baptism the Christian partner be deserted by the non-Christian, the Christian partner is free under the "privilegium Paulinum" to regard the existing marriage as dissolved and to marry again with any baptized Christian. It should be made clear under this head that the privilege only applies when the Christian partner has been deserted by the non-Christian. If the Christian drive away the non-Christian, he cannot claim it.

Since serious difficulties arise in places where Christian marriages are impossible, from the fact that no Christian partner is available, or from other grave reasons, and that in certain dioceses dispensations have in fact been issued in such cases, we consider that in the present state of the Church, the Bishop of a diocese, after due consultation, and subject to any rule of his Province, should, if he think fit, grant dispensation in such cases Such dispensation should be strictly limited to an individual case

If a Christian be united to a non-Christian by non-Christian rites without dispensation, it should be left to the Bishop to decide on the actual validity of the marriage in the eyes of the Church, and the nature of the discipline, if any, to be imposed. We do not say that such a marriage is necessarily invalid in every case.

If such a marriage be declared valid, it is consequently indissoluble on the side of the Christian. (If the non-Christian be eventually baptized, the parties to it should not be re-married, but the marriage should be blessed.) In this case the Christian, who being such had married a non-Christian, has no claim to the "Privilegium Paulinum" which applies solely to cases in which a married heathen becomes a Christian.

The marriage of a Christian with a Catechumen stands on a special footing, and must be treated in each Province in accordance with the status which is recognized in that Province as belonging to the Catechumenate

Holy Baptism.

Our reference includes "other practical questions" besides marriage. Two such subjects have been referred to us , the first is the question of the baptism of illegitimate children. We prefer to regard this as one application of a wider principle, and to say that it is undesirable that infants should be baptized

unless there is good assurance of their Christian upbringing,
but that where this is given, baptism should not ordinarily be
refused on other grounds. That what should be accepted
and considered such good assurance should be left to the authorities of the local Church.

The second is the case of persons alleged to have been baptized
with little or no preparation or instruction When there is a
doubt whether they were baptized at all the case is met by
conditional baptism, but when the persons in question are
troubled with doubts because of their lack of instruction and
faith, we recommend that when the *matter* and *form* of their
baptism have been duly verified, the opportunity of confirmation
be taken to supply what has been lacking and to allay anxiety.
In all cases of difficulty the Bishop would be the right person to
decide.

MISSIONS AND GOVERNMENTS.

Freedom to preach the Gospel of Christ in every country is
a right which must be claimed by Christians of every race and
nationality as being essential to their own spiritual life and the
fulfilment of their religious obligations The readiness with
which this right will be conceded will depend largely upon the
confidence in their " bona fides " which the missionaries can
inspire. It must be recognized, on the one hand, that governments have responsibilities which they must fulfil, and on the
other, that missionaries, though they cannot divest themselves
of nationality, are bound to make it plain that they place their
allegiance to Christ above every other allegiance and that they
will not jeopardize the extension of His Kingdom by abusing
the position which the recognition of the principle of religious
freedom has secured for them

The War had in certain cases sapped the foundations of this
confidence, and the imposition of some temporary restrictions
on the freedom of missionaries was inevitable In laying down
the conditions on which missionaries of alien nationalities shall
be at liberty to exercise their calling within the British Empire,
the Government has freely acknowledged the value of the work
done by Missions in the past, and cordially welcomed their
co-operation in the future, and has invoked the assistance of
National Missionary organizations to safeguard the interests
which it is bound to protect. We are glad to share in rendering
this assistance, believing that in this way we can help to restore
confidence, and hasten the time when we may reasonably claim
complete freedom for Missionary enterprise.

For a time German Missionaries have been excluded from
many fields till confidence can be restored We do not question
the necessity of this, but we feel deeply the loss which the

missionary cause has sustained by their removal from the field of their labours, and the spiritual loss both to them and the world at large which their enforced abstention from much of their missionary work must entail. We recognize it as a duty incumbent upon ourselves and them alike to work for the removal of those causes of mistrust to which this exclusion owes its origin. We cannot fail to recognize the serious influence which this action of the British Government may exercise upon other governments and would emphasize the fact that it is only as a *temporary* measure that we are required to submit to these restrictions: to accept them as *permanent* limitations of religious freedom would come perilously near to the repudiation of our primary Christian obligation.

In dealing with the large number of persons in their colonies and dependencies who profess different faiths, the policy of the British and American Governments has always been that of strict religious neutrality. We heartily endorse this policy, having no desire to see any kind of political influence brought to bear upon people to induce them to change their religion. But we cannot fail to notice that in certain instances the ferment produced among primitive races who have received the Gospel of Christ has led to hindrances being placed in the way of missionaries in the prosecution of their work, and to a preference being shewn for other faiths. The Church would be failing in her work if the acceptance of the truths did not awaken in her converts a higher sense of their dignity as human beings, of their rights as well as their duties, and any government which has the real interest of subject races at heart will be glad of such awakening even though, in civil life, it raises new problems to be solved.

We hold it to be the duty of missionaries to look at their work from the Government point of view, as well as from their own, and to adapt their methods, as far as is consistent with Christian morality and justice and with the Faith and Order of the Church, to the policy which the Government is following in dealing with such peoples. On the other hand, we claim that no discrimination should be shewn against the Christian Faith, and that the greatest care should be taken by public officials, lest they be betrayed into doing or saying anything which is bound to be interpreted by the people in a sense which does dishonour to our Lord. Further, we feel it is necessary to urge that the religious sentiments of Christians are entitled to be treated with the same consideration that is so markedly, and rightly, shewn to those of men professing other faiths.

In the present state of international relations there is a real danger that missionaries may be tempted to forward the commercial and political aims of their own nation, and we emphatically declare that such action lies entirely outside the scope of their proper functions.

The insistent demand on the part of subject races for self-government is one of the outstanding features of the times, and missionaries will sympathize strongly with the desire for self-expression which inspires it. The advisability or otherwise of giving public expression to this feeling will depend upon local conditions, but in no case should a missionary involve himself in the party politics which are inseparable from the pursuit of such an aim. In seeking to secure the removal of some great moral evil, the missionary may feel called upon to support the political party which has espoused this cause, but in doing so should make it clear that it is the moral and not the political issue at stake which has claimed his support. The opium traffic in China is such a moral question, and one which at the present time calls for the earnest attention of the Church. The Committee on International Relations has dealt with this subject, and accordingly we but refer to it by way of illustration.

In Eastern Countries as in the West, the Church has led the way in education, and in some lands still leads; there is a growing tendency, however, throughout the world for the State to claim the training of its future citizens as its own special function, and, being in some cases desirous to impress upon its subjects the stamp of its own peculiar culture, it has been reluctant to allow missionaries of other nationalities to take any part in this work. Christian missionaries, whatever their nationality may be, should recognize the duty of loyalty to the ruling power and its right to claim their co-operation in the development of the spirit of true citizenship. Christianity, as the universal religion, can find outward expression in various types of culture, while inspiring all with the same spirit.

The assumption of the work of education by the State with the national resources at its disposal, must render it difficult for Missions, if largely dependent, as they usually are, upon voluntary offerings, to maintain an equal standard of efficiency in an extensive system of schools, but we maintain that the Church has an ideal of education which it is bound to set forth, and the power of developing a type of manhood which no purely secular system can produce, and with which no State can afford to dispense. In the face of this changing situation, the need of shaping afresh the educational policy of missions is imperative, and for the ascertaining of the necessary data on which it may be based and the determination of the policy itself, the co-operation of Christians of all lands is essential. Isolated action is to be earnestly deprecated, for the true solution of a local problem is frequently only to be found when it is studied in relation to the whole problem of which it forms a part, and wrong action in one case may have a widespread influence, prejudicial to the general cause of education.

For concerted action some organization, both National and

International, is necessary, which while leaving untouched the independence of Missionary Societies will co-ordinate their thinking and activities. Such organizations can only work effectively so long as they enjoy the complete confidence of the Societies for whose assistance they exist, and herein lies the safeguard against their attempting to assume any coercive jurisdiction. Most valuable service was rendered by the Conference of Missionary Societies of the United Kingdom, and by the Foreign Missions Conference of North America during the War and at the Peace Conference, in safeguarding missionary freedom and saving German mission property from alienation to secular purposes. There is still work to be done in the councils of the nations, which can only be undertaken effectively by some central authority, and the League of Nations should find its counterpart in an International Missionary Conference. Such a Conference, as we have already indicated, would not confine its attention to safeguarding missionary freedom, but would help in shaping missionary policy. "Every solid question," a great thinker has said, "has at least four sides," and there is great gain in enlisting the best missionary minds from different nations for a joint endeavour to solve the problems which face the Church as it seeks to commend the Gospel to every Nation.

In conclusion we desire gratefully to acknowledge the great assistance we have received from :

The Rev Dr W. H. Frere, Rev. Dr Darwell Stone, Rev. Dr. F. E. Brightman, Rev. O. D. Watkins, Rev. Dr. Weitbrecht Stanton, the Rev. Father Puller, the Bishops of Moray and Ross, Vermont, Western New York, N.W. Australia, and Zanzibar, and J. H Oldham, Esq., who either by personal communication or written statement contributed valuable information, and tendered wise counsel concerning several of the subjects dealt with in our report.

(Signed) F. CALCUTTA,

Chairman.

No. V.

REPORT OF THE COMMITTEE † APPOINTED TO CONSIDER AND REPORT UPON THE POSITION OF WOMEN IN THE COUNCILS AND MINISTRATIONS OF THE CHURCH.

WE, appointed as your Committee to consider and report on the " position of Women in the Councils and Ministrations of the Church," have drawn up the following Report with a deep sense both of the difficulty and of the importance of the subject entrusted to us. The questions connected with the position of women in the life and in the work of the Church, through the events of the last few years, have had a new emphasis laid on them ; and they must be considered afresh in their new context. We are profoundly conscious that the Holy Spirit teaches Christian people by those age-long precedents which we believe to be the outcome of His guidance. But sometimes it becomes our duty, faithfully retaining the lessons of the sacred past, in a very special sense to trust ourselves to His inspiration in that present which is our time of opportunity, in order that He may lead us into whatsoever fresh truth of thought or of action is in accordance with the will of God. For the Holy Spirit is with us and with our generation no whit less than He was with our elder brethren in Christ in the first days of the Gospel.

The foundation of a right and stable view of the whole

† Names of Members of the Committee :—

Bishop of Aberdeen
Bishop of Arizona
Bishop of Ballarat
Bishop of Barbados
Bishop of Chester
Bishop of Columbia
Bishop of Coventry
Bishop of Edinburgh
Bishop of Ely (*Chairman*)
Bishop of Gippsland
Bishop of Grafton
Bishop of Hull (*Secretary*)
Bishop of Jamaica
Bishop of Kingston-on-Thames
Bishop of Leicester
Bishop of Lincoln
Bishop of Liverpool

Bishop of Lucknow
Bishop of New York
Bishop of Ossory
Bishop of Peterborough
Bishop Remington (South Dakota Suffragan)
Bishop of Rhode Island
Bishop of Sheffield
Bishop of Southern Florida
Bishop of Swansea
Archbishop of Sydney
Bishop of Tokyo
Bishop of Toronto
Bishop of Truro
Bishop of Uganda
Bishop of Western Michigan

subject must be laid in a review of the witness of that creative epoch in which first of all our Lord Himself lived on earth and taught, and in which later His Spirit was most conspicuously directing the thought and action of the Christian society. With deep reverence we recognize that the supreme ministry of redemption was wrought out by *One Who was a man*,* (ἀνήρ) Jesus Christ our Lord. It is certain that the Apostles were men; almost as certain that the Seventy were men. On the other hand a woman was chosen to be the handmaid of the Lord in the Incarnation of the Son of God. In our judgement there is nothing to prevent our believing that the Apostolic commission recorded in St. John xx. 19–23 was delivered to women as well as to men. In the parallel history (St. Luke xxiv. 33) we read that the two who came from Emmaus " found the eleven gathered together, and them that were with them." It seems impossible to argue that the last words (τοὺς σὺν αὐτοῖς) were meant to exclude women. In Acts i. 14 " the women and Mary, the mother of Jesus " are named as having part in the fellowship of the upper room. With Bishop Westcott and Dr. Hort we venture to think that the great commission was given to those who were representatives of the whole Church; and among those representatives we have every reason to think that women had a place. Again, we are led to conclude that the evangelistic charge (St. Matt. xxviii 16–20) was delivered to a company which included women. The words of the Evangelist are : " But the eleven disciples went away into Galilee, into the mountain where Jesus had appointed them. And when they saw Him they worshipped Him; οἱ δὲ ἐδίστασαν." The natural meaning of the last words is " but others doubted." Others then, we infer, beside the eleven were present; and if others, then we may say with great probability that women were among them. This probability is immensely increased if we identify, as there is strong reason for identifying, this appearance of the risen Lord with that of which St Paul tells us (1 Cor. xv. 6), the appearance to above 500 brethren at once. Demonstration in these as in so many other important matters is beyond our reach. But at least the strong probability is that women were among the recipients of the great commission and of the evangelistic charge, as afterwards they were of the gift of Pentecost.

We turn now to St. Paul. Two passages must be briefly considered. (*a*) In Gal iii 26–28 the Apostle wrote : " For ye are all sons of God, through faith, in Christ Jesus. For as many of you as were baptized into Christ did put on Christ. There can be neither Jew nor Greek, there can be neither bond nor free, there can be no male and female : for ye are all one

---

* Compare St. Luke xxiv. 19; Acts ii. 22, xvii. 31. What is said in the text above does not exclude the belief that in our Lord's human character there were manifested traits which are commonly feminine.

man in Christ Jesus." The passage quoted begins with the
assertion of the potential universality of sonship. It ends with
the assertion of the oneness of the body (εἷς ἐστέ). But quite
obviously the oneness of the body allows, indeed implies, diversity
of function. The passage does not touch the question of the
character of woman's functions in the Church It does not in
the least suggest that the functions of women are the same
as the functions of men It simply asserts that membership
in the one body is not restricted by race or by social status or
by sex. (b) It is often said that in his first Epistle to Corinth
St Paul is inconsistent, and various expedients are resorted to
in order to reconcile him with himself Let us look at the
passages themselves In xi. 5 the Apostle writes: "Every
woman praying or prophesying with her head unveiled dis-
honoureth her head." Here St. Paul assumes that there is nothing
wrong in a woman praying or prophesying; and prophesying
implies the presence of others. He takes it for granted that
women will do this. The great Pentecostal prophecy itself
foretold that "your daughters" as well as "your sons" "shall
prophesy"; and it is added that "upon my handmaidens"
will I "in those days pour forth of my Spirit." But in chapter xiv.
the context is wholly different. St. Paul is there speaking of the
ἐκκλησίαι, the public assemblies of the Church. "Let the
women keep silence in the assemblies it is shameful for a
woman to speak in the assembly" (compare 1 Tim. ii. 12).
In the assembly St. Paul contemplated the whole Christian
society in Corinth being gathered together (v 23); and, what is
far more important for our purpose, he expected that persons
ignorant of the faith and even that unbelievers—heathen men—
would find their way in. Those who were converts from the
worship of idols and those who still worshipped idols alike knew
only too well the shameful position which women took in the
heathen temples and their rites Corinth was a very bye-word for
vice. The Greeks coined a word "to corinthianize," meaning
thereby "to play the harlot" The female temple slaves were
simply prostitutes. At Corinth then in the Christian assemblies,
with their doors thrown open to all comers, St. Paul sternly said
that it was "shameful for a woman to speak." Here women must
set an example such as no one could question (to use the words of
the Pastoral Epistle) of "shamefastness and sobriety." Further,
what shall we say of St Paul's words in this passage about the
"subjection" of women? In our belief, as we have already
said, St Paul asserted the spiritual equality of men and women;
neither is afore or after the other. This spiritual equality will
be realized without let or hindrance in the spiritual world which
is to come. But in this present world of action between these
equals, man and woman, man has a priority, and in the last
resort authority belongs to him. As the world in which we live

becomes more like the world to come, this qualification becomes less and less operative, just as the stronger races assert their power in diminishing degree over their spiritual equals, the weaker races. In times such as that in which St. Paul wrote the necessary qualification became a predominating influence, and in this matter, as in the case of slavery, St Paul's teaching was conditioned by the existing circumstances of the world around him. He stooped to it that he might raise it. The statement then of what we believe to be the truth in regard to the human relations between men and women, as (we reverently say) in regard to the divine relations between the Persons within the Godhead, must needs take the form of a paradox Difference of function between man and woman in the Church, as in the world, and the relative subordination of the woman in no way imply an inferiority of woman in regard to man.

Our firm conviction is that the precise form which St. Paul's disciplinary directions took was relative to the time and to the place which he actually had in mind, but that these directions embody an abiding principle To transfer with slavish literalness the Apostle's injunctions to our own time and to all parts of our own world would be to renounce alike our inalienable responsibility of judgement and the liberty wherewith Christ has made us free. On the other hand it is our duty to endeavour clearly to discern the abiding law which underlay St Paul's stringent temporary and local rules We believe it to be this. Human nature being what it is, the Christian Church, whose duty and desire is to keep itself unspotted from the world, and to be like a home of brethren and sisters at unity with each other, must exercise unsleeping vigilance that in its regulations for worship in the congregation there lurk no occasion for evil or even for suspicion of evil, no occasion for confusion or strife; nothing which falls below the purest and strictest ideal of peace and seemliness and order.

It will be observed that in our terms of reference nothing is said about religious communities of women. That great subject therefore with its special problems lies outside our purview. But we cannot refrain from expressing our sense of the notable services they have rendered to the Church and to the world, and our hope and belief that God will be pleased to perfect that which He has begun in them and by them. We may be allowed to add one remark suggested to us by our slight contact with the subject. We believe that much good would result by a closer relationship between a community and the Bishop of the Diocese and by the creation of central advisory bodies, containing an ample representation of the communities themselves, which would promote co-ordination and mutual communication between the several communities

Before we pass to our proper task of dealing with the position of women in the Church first in relation to its Councils and then in relation to its Ministrations, there are two matters on which we desire to lay stress

In the first place, the Anglican Communion is spread throughout the world. It has many parts, and these parts are very diverse in character and that in many respects A Missionary Diocese is utterly different from a diocese which looks back over a continuous history of many centuries. One Church is established ; another has no relation to the State which differentiates it from all other religious bodies The political and social conditions which surround one Church are in marked contrast to those which surround another. Hence we give the advice, which as a Committee we are appointed to give, with the full consciousness not only that, if we may be forgiven for stating a truism, each constituent part of the Anglican Communion is absolutely at liberty to accept or to reject our counsel, but also that, even if it is accepted by all as essentially wise and right, yet all cannot equally and at once translate it into action. It is in this sense that we submit our conclusions to our brethren in the Conference and to the wider circle of all those throughout the world who are joined with us in the fellowship of the Anglican Communion.

Again, when we contemplate the position of women in the Church in the two relations indicated, we are led to believe that there are reasons for change in the custom of the Church, and that on the other hand there are reasons for caution

When we survey at any rate the recent history of some, if not all, parts of the Anglican Communion, we are obliged to confess that the Church has failed to treat women workers with generosity or even with justice It is a platitude to say that some of the very best work of the Church has been done, with singular patience and conscientiousness, with singular vigour and ability, with singular devotion to our Lord, by women But the women to whom we owe this great debt have received but scanty acknowledgement from the Church in the way either of actual salary or of recognition or of a responsible share in directing the activities or the policy of the Church either centrally or parochially.

It is now, we believe, generally, if not universally, recognized that the future must be different from the past. The education of women has advanced in a way which would have seemed incredible to our fathers. Witness the place which women take in the new and even in the ancient universities. Again, in most parts of our Communion the Church is in a new environment of social life which it is impossible for us to neglect. Women sit in legislative and in municipal assemblies They speak at public meetings on all manner of questions social, economic, political ; and that with a grasp of their subject of which the

women of a former generation would have been incapable. We
may see dangers in this revolution, but we cannot ignore it or
refuse to allow it a practical influence on our judgement. And,
further, within the Church we have seen an advance, great,
though not commensurate with that in secular matters. Within
the last few years many of us have watched the work of the
Pilgrims of Prayer and of the Women Messengers. We have noted
how these movements have stirred especially country parishes,
and have won in a remarkable degree general confidence. They
have shewn, past possibility of doubt, that women possess a won-
derful evangelistic gift In their addresses *cor ad cor loquitur*
Women also of mature judgement have spoken at mixed meetings
of men and women on the difficult and delicate subject of
sexual sin, its prevention and the rescue of its victims, with
sympathy, with power, with restraint. These are facts, and
we are convinced that, if the recognition of these facts is grudging
and inadequate, at least two evil results will ensue. We run a
grave risk of wasting a great power for spiritual good, which, as
many are profoundly convinced, it is the will of God that we
should use for His better service We also run the grave risk of
alienating from the Church, and even from Christianity, not a
few of those able and high-minded women before whom, if they
turn to social or educational work, there open out careers of
great and increasing responsibility.

On the other hand there are reasons for caution. We dare
not forget elementary facts of human nature. Women have the
power of moving men. By effective speech on religious truths
and experiences strong emotions are called into play. On
strong emotions possible perils wait. And, especially in a
generation which seems sometimes even contemptuously and
recklessly to brush aside what a very few years ago were regarded
as wise and indeed necessary restraints, the Church must be
above suspicion and must not fear to be watchful Again,
there is a deep wisdom in the words of the New Testament
which say of a faithful Christian woman "she shall be saved
through her child bearing" The Church, while fully acknowledging that some women are called to a life of celibacy, yet in
these days of a falling birth-rate and of all that that sinister
phenomenon implies, must not do anything which obscures or
renders difficult woman's fulfilment of her characteristic function
in human life. Again, looking at the whole position from
another point of view, we realize how heavy a responsibility
rests on the whole of our own Communion, and especially on its
rulers, to avoid any action which might retard the growth of
mutual recognition and regard between ourselves and other
historic branches of the Catholic Church. Lastly, while a real
advance as to the position of women is, we believe, not only
advisable but even necessary, we feel that the Church owes a duty

to all classes of its members, to those who are (as some may think) slow of movement as well as to those who are (as others may think) ambitious of revolutionary speed

We now turn to details And here we wish to record our gratitude for the assistance which we have received from memoranda placed in our hands, from interviews with certain representative women, from the Report (as yet unpublished) of a Committee appointed by the Archbishop of Canterbury to consider questions relating to the office of Deaconess, the Chairman of which was the Bishop of Chester, and from *The Ministry of Women* (a Report by a Committee appointed by the Archbishop of Canterbury, and presided over by Bishop Ryle, the Dean of Westminster). We have entirely relied upon this last named book, a work of wide research and learning, for information as to the facts of history.

(1) *The position of women in the Councils of the Church.*— In quite recent times there has been a very considerable advance in regard to the share assigned to women in the Councils of the Church. We may instance in England the " Rules for the Representation of the Laity " (under the " Church of England Assembly (Powers) Act "), which, after enumerating the various Assemblies—Parochial, Ruri-decanal, Diocesan, and the House of Laity in the National Church Assembly—adds the comprehensive direction " All representatives may be of either sex." But the advance made has not been uniform throughout the Anglican Communion Indeed, considering the great variety of conditions to which we have already alluded, such uniformity is impossible We have endeavoured carefully to consider the whole question, and we are strongly of opinion that to whatever Assemblies of the Church laymen are admitted, women should be admitted to the same on equal terms. For the sake of clearness we add that in making this recommendation we have in mind provincial or central Assemblies as well as those which are diocesan or parochial.

When this recommendation is acted on we have but one fear. We are conscious that there is a danger lest Churchmen should shirk their responsibilities and leave too heavy a share in the counsels of the Church to Churchwomen, as they have already too often done in the work of the Church In regard to the conduct of the business of the Church and to the determination of its policy we lay the utmost stress on the ideal of co-operation of Churchmen and Churchwomen ; and we believe that the attainment of this ideal, if only there is a conscientious response to the call of plain duty, lies well within the limits of what is possible.

(2) *Deaconesses.*—For the history of Deaconesses in the early centuries of the Church's life and for an account of their functions we must refer to the *Ministry of Women*. It is now about sixty years since, in the Anglican Communion, an effort arose to restore this ancient ministry. But this restoration has been carried out not on the authority of the several churches of our Communion, but rather on that of individual Bishops. The Church in the United States of America is an honourable exception to this statement ; for there among the Canons there is a section entitled " Of Deaconesses."

The result of this general informality of action is that a large measure of uncertainty prevails as to the status of a Deaconess and as to the conditions under which she exercises her functions. Is a Deaconess set apart for a religious office ? Or is she in the full sense of the word Ordained so that she possesses Holy Orders ? Again, can she lay down her office and thereby cease to be a Deaconess ? Or does she receive a " character " which is permanent ? Again, is a Deaconess at liberty to marry ? Or is she by a somewhat indefinite understanding pledged to celibacy ? We believe that the fact that it is not possible to give a clear and authoritative answer to these and other like questions has seriously retarded the growth of the diaconate of women among us ; for many of the best and ablest women, as we believe, shrink from joining a body the position of which is so ill-defined and precarious. We are persuaded that this period of tentative and provisional action ought now to come to an end, and that the time has arrived when in the interests of the Church at large and, in particular, of the Ministry of Women, the Diaconate (the revival of which ancient office was hailed with thankfulness by the Lambeth Conference of 1897) should be canonically and formally recognized in the several Provinces ; and our advice is that, so far as possible, the proper steps should be everywhere taken to secure the restoration of the Order of Deaconesses We lay stress on the word *restoration :* for what we recommend is not in any sense the creation of a new, but the constitutional restoration of an ancient, Ministry.

We pass to the fundamental question of the status of a Deaconess and of the nature of her ordination. In our judgement the ordination of a Deaconess confers on her Holy Orders. In ordination she receives the " character " of a Deaconess in the Church of God ; and, therefore, the status of a woman ordained to the Diaconate has the permanence which belongs to Holy Orders. She dedicates herself to a lifelong service.

But here at once there arises the grave question of the possibility of a Deaconess marrying. We are well aware that opinions on this subject differ, and many who hold the office of Deaconess desire that, though they have taken no vow of celibacy, marriage should be regarded as wholly out of the question for them. We have given the question our anxious consideration. And we record our deliberate belief that it ought plainly to be understood that no promise of celibacy is required for admission to the Order of Deaconesses. We recognize that a Deaconess who is married is likely to possess as a married woman a peculiar power by prayer and counsel to help married women ; and, that being so, we do not think that Deaconesses should be precluded from marrying. A married Deaconess might, especially during the earlier years of her married life, be compelled to ask the Bishop to allow her to suspend the actual exercise of some, if not all, of her functions. But she would retain the status of a Deaconess and, after an interval, would in most cases be able to resume her active work.

We desire to see in use in every branch of the Anglican Communion a Form and Manner of making of Deaconesses, such as might be fitly included in the Ordinal We assume that all such Forms of Ordination would be of the same general type, and so far as possible similar in their most significant parts, though varying in less important details in accordance with local needs and desires. In all of them there should be included provision for

(1) Prayer by the Bishop with the laying on of his hands ;

(2) A form of words to be said by the Bishop giving authority to execute the office of a Deaconess in the Church of God ;

(3) The delivery of the New Testament by the Bishop to each candidate.

Letters of Orders should be given to each Deaconess by the Bishop during or immediately after the ordination, and the names of those who are ordained should be duly entered by the Bishop's Registrar or Secretary in the Diocesan roll in like manner as the names of those who are ordained Priests and Deacons

We lay great stress on the requirement that each candidate should pass through a course of appropriate training, devotional, practical, and intellectual. Special attention should be paid to the study of the Bible, Christian doctrine, the Book of Common Prayer, and the history of the Church. It will be important to maintain a high standard in intellectual attainments Each candidate should be examined by persons well qualified for the work and appointed by the Bishop himself.

There is a considerable divergence of opinion as to the right age for admission to the Order of Deaconesses. On the one hand it is pointed out that women who have taken a degree at a University will desire as soon as possible after graduation to enter on the full exercise of the office to which they hope to dedicate their lives. On the other hand it is urged that the office of Deaconess requires a certain maturity in experience and character and is rather a goal of a term of service than of necessity its beginning. On the whole we think that the determining conditions will vary in the different parts of the Anglican Communion, and that the question of age is a subject best left for independent determination.

We spent much time and careful thought on the definition of the duties of a Deaconess. We are of opinion that the following functions may rightly be entrusted to the Deaconess :—

(1) To prepare candidates for Baptism and Confirmation ;

(2) To assist at the administration of Holy Baptism, and by virtue of her office to be the administrant of that Sacrament in cases of necessity ;

(3) Under such conditions as shall from time to time be laid down by the Bishop, and with the approval of the Parish Priest, (i) to render assistance at the administration of the Holy Communion to sick persons ; (ii) to read Morning and Evening Prayer and the Litany in Church, excepting such portions as are assigned to the Priest only , (iii) in Church also to lead in prayer and, under licence of the Bishop, to instruct and exhort the Congregation ;

(4) To pray with and to give counsel to such women as desire help in difficulties and perplexities.

Further, we are anxious that the office of Deaconess should be a standing witness that the Church welcomes workers of many kinds, and believes that a pure Christian intention hallows labours which are often regarded as secular. We therefore urge that, while a sufficient training in devotion and in doctrine must ever be considered as an indispensable element in the preparation of a Deaconess, Deaconesses and women looking forward to the Diaconate should be encouraged to qualify themselves for, and to take part in, work for public welfare, e g., educational, medical, or social. We should rejoice to see a Deaconess devoting much of her time to social or civic activities, provided she undertook those duties as part of her share in the great work of forwarding the Kingdom of God, and performed them in the name of Christ.

The attachment to the office of Deaconess of the functions which we have specified, so sacred, so intimately human, so conspicuously important, so wide in their range, is a sufficient indication that we regard, as we earnestly hope that Church-people generally will increasingly regard, that office as one to be held in reverence and honour.

Circumstances may arise, such as family reasons to which we alluded above, which would cause a Deaconess to desire to resign the exercise of her functions, at least for a time, though by that suspension of her activities she would not forfeit her status as a Deaconess. In such a case she should in our judgement apply to the Bishop of the Diocese in which she has been licensed. Further, we recommend that the Bishop of the Diocese in which a Deaconess is serving shall have power to suspend her from the exercise of her office and for grave reason to deprive her of her Orders as a Deaconess, the right of appeal in the latter case being duly safeguarded.

We are conscious that many other matters must be determined, if the Order of Deaconesses is to make its full contribution to the life of the Church. But we think that we have dealt with the great principles which are of universal application. Other questions must be determined in the several Dioceses and Provinces of the Anglican Communion

We desire to call attention to one further matter before we turn from the subject of the restoration of the Order of Deaconesses in the Anglican Communion. The question will certainly be asked whether we have any ulterior object in the proposals which we have made. We have not. We believe that for Women the Order of Deaconesses is the one and only Order of the Ministry which has the stamp of Apostolic approval (Rom xvi. 1, 1 Tim. iii, 11), and for Women it is the one and only Order which we can recommend that our Branch of the Catholic Church should recognize and use.

(3) *Laywomen* —In the last place we have endeavoured to give careful consideration to the question of the ministrations of laywomen, that is, of women other than Deaconesses We desire to lay down the principle that with regard to lay people speaking both in consecrated and in unconsecrated buildings the same opportunities under the same conditions should be given to women as to men We also think that in Churches as well as elsewhere at services other than the regular and appointed services of the Church laywomen should have the opportunity of leading in prayer

We realize that in carrying out in practice the recommendation which we have just formulated there will be some necessary variation under the very different conditions prevailing in the several parts of the Anglican Communion We assume that everywhere women will exercise the ministries which we have above assigned to them with the approval of the Bishop of the Diocese and of the Parish Priest, and under such conditions as shall from time to time be laid down by the Bishop.

We have above equated the opportunities of speaking in consecrated buildings offered to laymen and to laywomen. Among men the habitual exercise of this function is practically confined to those who have been admitted to the office of Readers. An analogy therefore is bound to grow up between the Lay Readers who are men and the women who are entrusted with similar duties. In this context therefore we venture to put on record our opinion that the time has come when the regulations as to Lay Readers (whose devoted work we gratefully acknowledge) should everywhere be made more definite and precise ; and in particular that it is urgently needful that everywhere the standard required of men who are to be admitted to the office of Lay Reader should be raised We think it our duty to emphasize the importance of carrying out as soon as possible this reform, so essential to the spiritual efficiency of the ministry of lay people.

As we are bidden to make recommendations which shall apply to all parts of the Anglican Communion, we find it impossible effectively to deal with the more general activities of women workers in the Church. Such activities are called out by local needs and are shaped by local circumstances. We cannot let this opportunity pass without expressing our sense of the great blessing such work has brought to multitudes of our people. What however at this moment we feel bound to note is, that women so working are always in danger of becoming isolated and of losing the strength and the larger vision which are the outcome of a wider recognition than that of a Parish We believe that the security against these possible evils and defects lies in Diocesan organization ; and that this security would be provided by a recommendation we put forward which deals with the whole range of women's work in the Church and with which we conclude our Report. We submit that in every Diocese there ought to exist a Board of Women's Work, including among its members men as well as women This Board would endeavour both to inspire and to direct women workers of all kinds within the Diocese All approved women workers would be placed upon its roll It would be ready to give them counsel. It would arrange for Retreats and Quiet days, and take other measures for building up the spiritual life of those who bear a heavy strain of work and difficulty and sometimes of disappointment. It would advise and encourage those younger women who are considering the call to Church work But among its other functions this Board would always include these two It would draw up and carry out a scheme whereby certificates of ascertained fitness and competence, recognized at least throughout the Diocese, would be given to women workers qualified in various departments of work. And in the second place it would from time to time consider the questions relating to the training of all women workers in the Church and the conditions of their employment and also to the remuneration of paid women workers in the Church By such an organization we are persuaded that their position would be raised and rendered more honourable, and that their efficiency, on which so much depends in the coming years, would be made more uniform and more stable.

(Signed)   F. H. ELY,

Chairman.

No. VI.

Report of the Committee† Appointed to Consider and Report upon Problems of Marriage and Sexual Morality.

Your Committee appointed to consider "Problems of Marriage and Sexual Morality" begs leave to report as follows:

In approaching the great problems of Marriage, Birth Control, and Sexual Purity we are conscious that we are called upon to deal with subjects of immeasurable importance to the human race, and concerning which nations and individuals look with longing desire for the help and guidance of the Christian Church. We are moved by a sympathy which comes from the knowledge that the temptations to sexual sin are probably the most universal in the world, and by the conviction of our own experience that it is the example and power of our blessed Lord's perfect humanity, with the gift of His Holy Spirit, which enables men to stand firm in hours of trial.

Therefore, in submitting our Report and the accompanying Resolutions, our hope is that our recommendations may be regarded not as the outcome of cold ecclesiasticism, but as the warmhearted effort of experience to guide and to sustain alike those who work for souls, those who long to see nations fit for their

† Names of Members of the Committee:—

Bishop of Bangor
Bishop of Birmingham
Bishop of Derry
Bishop of Dover
Bishop of Duluth*
Bishop of Edmonton
Bishop of Guildford (*Secretary*)
Bishop Howells
Bishop of Huron
Bishop of Kansas
Bishop in Khartoum*
Bishop of Lewes
Bishop of Llandaff
Bishop of London (*Chairman*)
Bishop of Nagpur
Bishop of Nassau
Bishop of North-West Australia
Bishop of Norwich
Bishop of Ottawa

Bishop of Rangoon
Bishop of Riverina*
Bishop of Sacramento
Bishop of St. Edmondsbury and Ipswich
Bishop of Singapore
Bishop of Sodor and Man
Bishop of Southampton
Bishop of Southwell
Bishop of Texas
Bishop of Thetford
Bishop of Vermont
Bishop of Victoria, Hong Kong
Bishop of Western Massachusetts
Bishop of Western Missouri
Bishop of Western Nebraska
Bishop of Willochra
Bishop of Zululand*

great world responsibilities, and those who know that they cannot fulfil God's purpose unless they have learned, whether in married or in single life, to be straight and clean before God and man.

The Christian Church has a code of morals as imperious in its claims as the rule of faith given in the Creeds. The Clergy are commissioned to teach the Christian Religion, which is to guide and hallow men's lives. To bear witness to the Divine Will, and to work for the fulfilment of that Will in the elevation and perfection of human life, is the very purpose of the Church's existence in the world. If the Church is to leaven human society, it must faithfully uphold this standard at any cost, both by its teaching and by the exercise of discipline, refusing the privileges of the Church to those who transgress the divine commandment. This witness is the duty not only of Bishops and Priests, or of the Church collectively in synod or convention, but of individual Christian people. Laws to be enforced, whether ecclesiastical or civil, must have a background of public opinion. Hence the great importance of being rightly informed as to the Christian law in this as in other matters, as well as of faithfulness and courage in bearing witness to it.

All will agree that there can be no subjects of graver importance than those connected with the sacredness of the family. The family is God's first institution upon earth, the cradle alike of Church and State, and marriage is the foundation of the family Where family life is dishonoured, wedded unfaithfulness lightly regarded, parental responsibility neglected, filial respect and obedience slighted, there, we may be sure, society is rotten at the core. We tremble for the future of a state or nation where lax theories concerning domestic life gain ground. Even laxer practice will certainly prevail.

There is sad evidence at the present time of a widespread lowering of moral conditions

The increased number of illegitimate births, accompanied by a lowered total birth-rate ; the multiplication of divorces, among the consequences of which the breaking up of homes for the children is not the least disastrous ; the widespread existence of venereal diseases, acquired or congenital, affecting a large percentage of the population ; these all sound a note of serious alarm and warning.

It is easy in this, as in other matters, to throw blame upon the war. To a large extent, and with some aggravations, the war probably disclosed conditions already existing, to which people generally were accustomed to shut their eyes.

We are persuaded that a great deal of the evil in question is due to ignorance, both of natural laws and of Christian teaching on the subject. And for this the Church must take its full share of blame in having failed to give plain teaching about marriage, and, before this, about purity Our young people and children must be taught the virtue of purity in the right and reverent treatment of their own bodies and in the relation of the sexes one to the other Purity should be taught not in a merely negative aspect as a refraining from wrongful indulgence, but as a positive virtue, shewn in the use of our nature, and its every part, for its intended purpose Whatever there may have been to say in the past in favour of a policy of silence on such subjects, the time for such a policy is now gone As a matter of fact, knowledge and discussion of matters of sex are far more widely spread than people generally recognize Children often in early years learn evil in all sorts of ways Guilty knowledge ought to be anticipated by wholesome training, in which modesty and reserve are carefully guarded It is a duty and privilege of fathers and mothers to give such instruction to their boys and girls This parental teaching should be supplemented by guardians, godparents, teachers—ordinarily of their own sex—and clergymen. These must qualify themselves for giving such guidance and instruction, whether individually or in the class or congregation. Each of these methods has its proper place. Educational authorities should be urged to interest themselves in the matter, and to use as may be found possible the influence and capacity of the teachers. In all such instruction care should be taken to train the character of the child as well as to give information in regard to these subjects. The dignity of purity, of a clean upright life, and the possibility of its preservation by the help of God through prayer and the sacraments, must be put before the young.

In connexion with the prescribed preliminaries of marriage, the Committee strongly urges that every effort should be made to impress upon those who are going to be married the importance of the step they are taking and its solemnity Courtship should be lifted to a higher level, and in particular betrothal should be presented to young people as a sacred matter. We feel that it is incumbent upon the clergy in every possible case to visit the betrothed persons, and to press upon them the responsibilities of marriage, and the sacredness of the union for which they are preparing

The Clergy are urged, as a part of their regular instruction in the Christian religion, to give to their people plain teaching and explanation about marriage, concerning which many are lamentably ignorant. For instance, they should insist on such fundamental principles as these :

(1) The *law* of marriage. Marriage according to God's design, to which we are recalled by our Lord Jesus Christ, is the

lifelong union of one man with one woman, to the exclusion of all others on either side. It is the union of two persons for the whole and every part of their life which justifies and hallows their physical union.

(2) While the *essence* of marriage consists in the consent before others of the man and woman to live permanently one with another as husband and wife, the Christian Church solemnizes the contract made in the presence of its minister with appropriate prayers and blessing.

(3) The *conditions* of marriage laid down by the civil authority must be complied with before the Church can solemnize a marriage. The Church may impose further conditions for its sanction and benediction.

(4) The *purposes* of marriage. Marriage is intended for the hallowing and control of natural sexual instincts ; for the procreation of children, and their nurture and training ; and for the mutual companionship and support of husband and wife in good and evil estate. To ignore or defeat any of these purposes is a violation of God's institution.

Clergymen often find their own judgement and experience quite inadequate for answering some of the questions, or for dealing with some of the cases, with which they may be faced in the course of their pastoral work. Much harm may be done by men of the best intentions through lack of knowledge as to the principles upon which their counsel should be based, or the way in which it should be given. The systematic study of Moral Theology ought to be regarded as an indispensable part of training for the Clergy, in order that they may have for their guidance, in the application of Christian principles to particular problems, the formulated experience of those who have given most consideration to the difficulties involved. It is greatly to be hoped that some standard work on this subject may be compiled by Anglican writers which will be accepted as embodying the Church's teaching in the light of present-day needs.

With regard to the permanence of marriage, our Lord's teaching, recalling men to God's original design for marriage, is given by St. Mark. " From the beginning of the creation male and female made He them. For this cause shall a man leave his father and mother and shall cleave to his wife ; and the two shall become one flesh ; so that they are no more two, but one flesh. What therefore God hath joined together let no man put asunder . Whosoever shall put away his wife and marry another committeth adultery against her : and if she herself shall put away her husband and marry another she committeth adultery." (St. Mark x 6–12. Cf. St. Luke xvi. 18 ; 1 Cor. vii,

10, 11.) This has been generally recognized as the principle
and standard which the Church of Jesus Christ is bound to
maintain. Although there has been from early times a difference
of opinion as to the meaning of our Lord's words as recorded in
St Matthew (v 32 and xix 9), and as to the lawfulness of
remarriage after divorce for the cause of adultery, the Committee
would earnestly urge that the only true standard of marriage,
which should be steadfastly upheld, is a lifelong union, for better
for worse, not shutting out the possibility of penitence and
reconciliation even after grievous offences.

Nevertheless, we admit the right of a National Church to deal
with the excepted case recorded in St. Matthew under such safeguards and disciplinary provisions as such Church may lay down.

Recognition of a single exception to the rule of indissoluble
marriage, "for the cause of adultery," with the disallow-
ance of any other causes that may be considered analogous
to this, rests on the fact that sexual unfaithfulness stands in a
different position from any other suggested ground of divorce,
since it is the perversion of a special and singular relation which
has no proper place outside the marriage tie.   This is not to make
little of the spiritual aspects of marriage of which the physical
union is a pledge and expression. Our Lord's words in St.
Matthew cannot be taken as giving only one sample out of many
sufficient causes for the dissolution of marriage, since none other,
however deplorable, touches the root of marriage itself   No
compassion for present hardships in particular cases can justify
the lowering for all of the standard of Christ, which alone insures
the welfare of society and of the race.

Discrepancy between civil law, made by and for persons of all
beliefs or of none, and that of the Christian Church, is often the
cause of difficulty as to the solemnization by the Church of a
marriage, which, though allowed by the State, is not in accordance
with the Church's law, and concerning the admission of the parties
thus married to the Sacraments and privileges of the Church.

If allowance is not made for such discrepancy, the acceptance
of universal civil marriage, followed, where this is sought, by the
Church's benediction, might have to be contemplated. For no
Christian Minister can suffer himself to be regarded simply as a
State official bound to perform or recognize any marriage which
the civil law allows. But this would not be, as is sometimes
supposed, an easy means of escaping from all complications
The Church's treatment of persons only civilly married would
raise innumerable questions of great perplexity. The Church is
better able to make its voice heard in this whole matter in some
parts of the world than in others, and the acquiescence of the
Church in civil marriage in any of the Home countries might react
unfavourably in the mission field. In all cases of civil marriage

it is desirable that the ceremony should be performed in a manner befitting the solemnity of the act. The Committee deems it very important that marriage preliminaries, whether ecclesiastical or civil, should be made more satisfactory than they are in many places at the present time. The preliminaries are supposed to insure delay, caution and publicity, but it is more than doubtful whether, generally speaking, they achieve their end.

With regard to the right use of marriage, difficult questions are forced upon our consideration. The purposes for which marriage is ordained have already been stated. It is not for us to deal with the strictly medical discussions on the subject, though these have engaged our careful attention. We recognize that the physical union of husband and wife has a sacramental value by which is expressed and strengthened the love that the one ought to have for the other. At the same time we urge the paramount importance in married life of deliberate and thoughtful self-control and we feel called upon to utter an earnest warning against the use of any unnatural means by which conception is frustrated. We are aware that many persons of undoubted sincerity, whose opinions are entitled to respect, do not share this view, considering the whole matter as chiefly a question of expediency to be determined on medical, financial and social grounds. This contention we cannot admit, as we believe that the question cannot be separated from the moral and religious issues involved.

The appalling statistics concerning the wide spread of venereal disease, reaching in its effect far beyond the person of the offender, forbid us to be silent on the subject. While moved by the most earnest desire to stop the disease, to cure those who have sinned, and in particular to protect the innocent from suffering, the Committee must condemn the distribution, or use before exposure to infection, of so-called prophylactics, since these cannot but be regarded as an invitation to vice. Subsequent treatment of those who have unhappily fallen is an entirely different matter, and should be encouraged and supported.

The Committee would urge that everywhere relentless warfare should be waged on brothels and on all who are directly or indirectly responsible for them, and likewise feels bound to protest against vice being in any way legalized, regulated or arranged for. In these matters the woman's side is to be considered as well as the man's. Women must not be sacrificed for the supposed benefit of men ; while for men we contend that such provision is neither necessary nor allowable. From the exhaustive research by Mr. Abraham Flexner it is manifest that even the object aimed at, of making vice safe, is not attained by licence and regulation, since under this system the evil with its consequences of disease is increased rather than diminished.

The wise and firm administration of laws relating to street solicitation, by men or women, should be insisted on. Parks and places of public recreation should be guarded for their proper use and preserved from becoming centres of demoralizing indecency. The employment of women police has in many places been found of great value and deserves the warm support of the Church. In the matter of seduction the age of consent should nowhere be lower than 18 years.

All such repression of wrong, it must be continually remembered, will be of little effect without a heightened public opinion penetrated by religious motives. The fear of God, whose displeasure at sins of impurity is constantly manifested in our experience, as well as recorded in Holy Scripture ; personal devotion to our Lord Jesus Christ, the model of true manhood ; and trust in the renewing power of the Holy Spirit—are needed to enable men and women to withstand the lusts of the flesh and to present their bodies to God a reasonable, holy and living sacrifice. Along with these higher motives we may plead with men for a chivalrous treatment of all women as of their own mothers, sisters and daughters, and with women for such self-respecting care in matters of dress and behaviour as will claim the respect of men and avoid any putting of stumbling-blocks in their way. All right-minded persons should be urged to unite in the suppression of pernicious literature and of plays, pictures and films suggestive of evil.

Complaints have been made of the low moral tone of Europeans and Americans which sometimes exist with regard to the treatment of Asiatic women and those of other races. There are places where immoral relations with them on the part of foreigners are too commonly regarded as allowable, while with white women they would be severely censured No such distinction of race or colour can be tolerated by the Christian Church One law must be maintained of purity and respect for all. At the same time the Committee recognizes the severe temptations to which young men employed in Eastern and tropical countries are exposed, at a distance from their families. We would urge, among other ameliorative measures, the reconsideration, in view of these moral dangers, of unduly severe restrictions sometimes imposed on their marriage.

Sad ignorance and apathy exist among Church people concerning Preventive and Rescue Work. Even in some of our congregations, where missionary interest is keen, the rescue work of the Church is never mentioned. The clergy themselves often-

I

times manifest a strange ignorance of actual conditions and a lack of sympathy with the efforts being made. What a contrast this to the mind of Christ as expressed in the Gospels! In witnessing for purity, and in restoring those who have fallen victims to sins of impurity, there is an urgent need for enlisting fresh forces. A larger number of educated women endowed with power of discernment and with wide sympathies is called for. In connexion with efficient workers there is need of central Homes for specialized training for this department of work to be carried on, both at home and in the mission field. The aid of a trained woman worker for advice and for organization has been found of the greatest value in a large number of dioceses, and is recommended for wider adoption.

In the care of those who have sinned methods of repression are largely discredited. It is recognized that the beauty and happiness of a Christian life should be put before them, and represented in the cheerful surroundings of the Home and in a living Christian fellowship, along with the discipline which is needed for building the character. For wise treatment greater classification is necessary. Young and old offenders cannot be helpfully gathered together in one Home. The feeble-minded need separate care. Maternity cases must be provided for, with the after-care of mother and child. All this involves a large outlay, but not more than offerings of love and penitence ought without difficulty to provide.

Hitherto the emphasis has been put chiefly on the results of immorality, and that mostly on the women's side. More thought should be given to the building up of pure manhood and womanhood, whereby both God will be glorified and the commonwealth be served.

There has been too general an acquiescence in the degrading lie that chastity is not to be expected in boys and men. The single standard for both sexes, before and after marriage, must be constantly insisted upon. It can be triumphantly pointed to as realized in the lives of multitudes of men and women.

The aid of men of good and disciplined character is needed for the help of boys and young men, and in combating horrible temptations to which they are often exposed from elders of their own sex. The Committee is compelled to notice the prevalence in some quarters of unnatural vice. The strengthening of general sentiment in abhorrence of such practices is of the greatest importance. We fear that the public conscience is not sufficiently alive to this terrible mischief.

Girls and boys are frequently drawn astray through the loneliness and dulness of their lives. As preventive measures, healthy amusements ought to be provided and opportunities afforded for friendly intercourse. We urge that by every kind of social effort men and women will strive to turn the loneliness of many lives into the brightness which should belong to Christian fellowship.

In the whole matter of combating impurity the co-operation of civic authorities should be sought as well as of medical men

While preventive and rescue work must be done as a rule on denominational lines, we strongly urge that for the preservation of public morals and raising the standard in a community, all religious denominations, and indeed all men of goodwill, should be invited to unite. Such unity and co-operation increases immensely the force of a moral protest, and by experience it has been found that few moral evils can stand for long before real united action. It is clear, moreover, that a council which represents all right-minded citizens has far more power in prosecuting the publishers and vendors of indecent literature, in clearing parks and open spaces of undesirable characters, and in attacking the at present unchecked scandal of the open sale in some places of contraceptives. It is hoped that some form of Public Morality Council, by whatever name it may be called, may be established in every large city, with local branches to deal with the ever-varying local forms of evil A Social Service Council in each country or state, such as exists in Canada, would be of great value in bringing the combined pressure of different religious bodies to bear upon legislative and administrative measures affecting moral interests.

It is only by the creation of a healthy public opinion that we can hope to get rid of many temptations which unnecessarily beset the path of our young people, and it is the duty of the Church to lead and foster such healthy public opinion throughout the world

(Signed)   A F. LONDON:

Chairman

No. VII.

REPORT OF THE COMMITTEE† APPOINTED TO CONSIDER AND REPORT UPON THE CHRISTIAN FAITH IN RELATION TO (a) SPIRITUALISM; (b) CHRISTIAN SCIENCE; AND (c) THEOSOPHY.

IT has been our task to consider the relation of the Christian Faith and the duty of the Church towards those movements of thought and practice which are associated at the present time with Spiritualism, Christian Science and Theosophy. Many of us have for some time studied much of the literature on one or all of the subjects; the published literature has formed the basis of this report, some of us have also taken opportunities of discussion with those who have special knowledge. It need not be said that our first aim is to be able to understand them at their best, to make sure that we have not overlooked or mis-represented important or salient features At the same time it is exceedingly difficult to achieve this end. The literature itself is voluminous : and at the same time it is not easy to find authoritative statements to enable us to define precisely the marks which distinguish the teaching and practice to be accepted by adherents We are told that Theosophy is a body of truths, but that members of the Theosophical Society are not bound to accept any particular statement of them. It is true that Christian Scientists are provided with a book which defines the content of their beliefs : but here again it is difficult to be sure that we appreciate correctly their use of the terms employed; for instance, are we meaning the same thing, or anything like the same thing, when we discuss the terms " reality," " error," " material," " spirit " or " the Christ " ?

† Names of Members of the Committee.—

Archbishop of Armagh	Bishop Nash (Capetown Coadjutor)
Bishop of Asheville	Bishop of Newcastle
Bishop in Assam	Archbishop of Nova Scotia
Bishop of Barrow (*Secretary*)	Bishop of Ossory
Bishop of Barbados*	Bishop of Ottawa
Bishop of Derby	Bishop of Quincy
Bishop of Exeter	Bishop of Oxford (*Chairman*)
Bishop of George*	Bishop of Sierra Leone
Bishop of Glasgow	Bishop of Southwark
Bishop of Goulburn	Bishop of Stafford
Bishop of Grafton*	Bishop Stearly (Newark Coadjutor)
Bishop of Grahamstown	Bishop of Tuam
Bishop of Jarrow	Bishop of Victoria, Hong Kong
Bishop of Kensington*	Bishop of Virginia
Bishop of Knaresborough	Bishop of Wakefield
Bishop of Kootenay	Bishop of Western New York
Bishop of Lincoln*	Bishop of West Virginia
Bishop of Llandaff	Bishop of Wyoming
Bishop of Madras	

However, we are able to appreciate characteristics common to all three subjects. First, they protest against materialism and a materialistic basis of human life. As in previous periods of human thought, so now this protest is the natural outcome of an epoch of ferment and unrest, and of immense material expansion accompanied by increasing facilities of communication, and by the rapid dissemination of ideas. In the Nineteenth century the development and the range of scientific discovery were stupendous : this tended at first to rivet popular attention upon the application of discoveries to promoting the material facilities and conveniences of life, and at the same time to encourage the belief that all the mysteries of life were discoverable and could be explained by theories derived from and verified by sense-observation. There followed inevitably the recognition of limitation and a sense of dissatisfaction, and it would be true to say that all departments of human speculation have been turned more and more in the direction of relating man and the world in which he lives to God, of recognizing the reality of the unseen, and of a deep longing for some revelation of it. Upon all this has come the catastrophe and shock of the War and the desolating, bewildering questions which such an experience raises. It is easy to understand the appeal which in times like our own the Spiritualist, the Christian Scientist and the Theosophist make, especially to those who may have been indifferent to the spiritual claim of religion and religious motives or absorbed in material interests.

Secondly, all three movements draw much of their strength from a new knowledge of the extent of psychic powers with which human nature is endowed. It seems that these powers are as real as, though less general than, our physical powers, and further, that the use or abuse of them depends in the same way upon spiritual control and direction. This is plainly shewn by the use and abuse of psychic gifts in the Bible story. Indiscriminate exercise of them is often just as fatal to the individual and to society as uncontrolled use of physical powers. Until it becomes clearer how such psychic powers may be rightly used and controlled, the Church is supported by psychologists in advising the greatest caution and restraint.

Thirdly, each of the three movements claims to supply something which the teaching and practice of the Church fail to give, whether in directness and correspondence with human needs of to-day or in comprehensiveness. Here they make their appeal to professed members of the Church who, for whatever reason, are left unsatisfied by the normal teaching and discipline offered to them

Fourthly, there is nothing essentially new in these particular movements, either in the circumstances which have stimulated them, or in the ideas which they express, or in the teaching which is given. It is not difficult, for instance, to recognize a revival of the doctrines, sometimes couched in the same terms, of the Gnostics and the Neo-Platonists, with the same developments of spiritualistic practice and the same distortions of it by the ignorant or the unscrupulous.

Fifthly, none of these movements finds its centre in the central revelation of the Christian Faith, namely the Incarnation of our Lord as the unique fact of human history and the means as well as the manifestation of redemption. Spiritualism practised as a religious cult appears generally to be independent of it : Christian Science seems to allegorize it or to allow it to fade into a false mysticism : Theosophy loses sight of it in a fusion of various religious systems.

We are therefore challenged now as in previous ages to fulfil as guardians of the Faith our natural office. We do not mean that we have merely to repeat time-honoured formulae. We have to state, and to state in terms which are real and convincing to the mind of our time, the fundamental truths of the Christian revelation, and following from them the purpose of our life here, its discipline, its hope, and its bearing upon a life beyond. Let it be said that one condition on which these truths become convincing is that the statement of them should be enriched by all the knowledge available. As has been said of Origen, so it must always be said of guardians of the Faith, "his faith was catholic and therefore he welcomed every kind of knowledge as tributary to its fulness." We are able wholeheartedly and without shrinking to welcome research, criticism, scientific investigation : we are ready to accept conclusions to the extent and within the limits which scientific reasoning and methods authorize. We have to safeguard ourselves and others against the inevitable tendency to allow the imagination to be caught by theories, and to translate them into practice, before we are sure of the grounds upon which they rest. Above all it is only by keeping firm hold of the cardinal truths upon which Christian faith and practice are established that new knowledge can be given its right setting.

THE CHRISTIAN FAITH IN RELATION TO

(a)—SPIRITUALISM.

It seems that in dealing with this subject on behalf of the Conference we have to address ourselves to two distinct questions : (1) What have we to say to the investigations of the phenomena of human consciousness and the results of those investigations conducted for a period of years, beginning in 1876, when Sir W. Barrett brought the subject of thought-transference or telepathy before the British Association, and carried on notably by the Society of Psychical Research ? (2) What have we to say to the religious cults and practices which have been created on the basis of what is believed to have been so far discovered and is known as Spiritualism ?

In answering the first question we say without hesitation that we welcome scientific investigation : we recognize the patience and the skill with which members of the Psychical Research Society examine the mass of evidence of all kinds submitted to them, and above all the unmistakeable desire to safeguard the inquiry against illusion or fraud, to arrive at truths, and to interpret scientific facts correctly. It is not for us to decide whether the scientific methods applied to these particular phenomena are appropriate, i.e. whether the methods of physical science can be applied to psychical phenomena. Our desire is to understand what conclusions have been reached along these lines of research. These have been stated as follows :

(1) There is a conviction of the reality of telepathy, or communication between living beings by means which appear to be independent of the normal sense-organs.

(2) There is also a conviction of the reality of a subconsciousness which may operate without the control of the normal consciousness and will (e.g. in dreams).

(3) This does not necessarily imply communication with beings no longer limited by the conditions of bodily existence as we know it here, but there are phenomena which appear to support that hypothesis.

(4) In investigating such phenomena great difficulties arise owing to the play, very imperfectly understood, of the subconscious self in the medium employed and in the inquirer. Mrs. Henry Sidgwick writes : " Before we can convince the world we not only want more cases giving evidence of the fact of personal survival but we want them solidly based on more knowledge of the subliminal self and the way it works, more knowledge of the conditions and process of telepathy, more understanding of the limitations under which communication with the dead occurs."

The outcome of these conclusions from the scientific side would seem to be :—

(1) To give a serious warning against unregulated and undue exercise of an element of human consciousness which acts independently of the reason and the will, and against allowing reason and will to abdicate in its favour.

(2) To insist upon an outlook upon life which refuses to accept materialism as a sufficient account of phenomena, and to encourage belief in a spiritual explanation.

We welcome inquiry conducted in this reverent and scrupulous spirit.

In answering the second question we enter on our main and proper function, which is to consider the religious cult and practice of what is called Spiritualism We have evidence that, especially under the stress of the horrors and anxieties of the war, particularly in our crowded areas, Spiritualism has affected in some instances even regular Church-goers, withdrawing them from the Church But it has mainly laid hold of that large class amongst us who have been casual in religious observance, and have never grasped or made their own the Christian teaching which rests upon the revelation gradually unfolded in the Bible, summed up in the Creed, and realized for us here in Sacraments. It deals with man's fellowship with God, and therefore with immortality, eternal life and the life we share with those who have passed from us. Many have felt and expressed dissatisfaction with the consolations offered by the Church, have misrepresented—no doubt unconsciously—what the Church holds and teaches, and have imagined that Spiritualist doctrine supplies something which the Church lacks and which the spirit of man needs to strengthen and uplift it. This shews that we have failed to teach clearly enough or fully enough the great simple Christian truths about the supernatural, and the grounds upon which those truths are based. We think there is real need now and in the immediate future to use the opportunities provided abundantly by the Press as well as in other ways to make clear and definite statements of what Christianity holds and hands on about the life of the world beyond and our relation to it during our life here.

Any such statement will insist that our view of life essentially centres in God , that the purpose of man's life here, or hereafter, is to attain fuller knowledge of God, a deeper, richer love of God, and a closer union with His Being ; that Jesus Christ is not only Himself Eternal God but also the one Mediator, through His Incarnation and Redemption, by whom man can reach God : that by His life in us, and by our life in Him we become sons of God : that the Sacraments convey to us the grace of God : that revelation through the prophets is the unfolding to us of the Wisdom of God   that the Eucharist is the method by which, through union with Jesus Christ, we may arise to God   Our duty and relation to one another rests upon the dependence of all of us upon God. The whole faith, strength, hope, activity of a Christian centres in the Love of God which is in Christ Jesus shed abroad in our hearts by the Holy Spirit to comfort and support us ; and God's Love holds together in constant fellowship those who share that Love here and those who have passed beyond

Spiritualistic religion and practice throw a wholly different emphasis upon the motive power of man's life : immortality is there concerned with the survival of human persons more than with God ; the life beyond is represented largely as an extension of what is experienced here and now ; and the fact is overlooked that survival is not necessarily immortality, still less eternal life

But, further, the Christian Faith declares that the life in Christ after death is an advance towards a more perfect fellowship with God for those who have been seekers after God and have not alienated themselves from fellowship with Him. That fellowship we may enjoy imperfectly here through the eternal life on which we have entered and in virtue of which by the grace of God we are enabled to respond to Him. We insist that conduct and the working out of character in the ordeal of life here is of vital importance in determining the condition under which we may enjoy fellowship with God hereafter.

In its doctrine of the Communion of Saints the Church insists that we can and do have Communion with the departed through the Love of God which is in Christ Jesus. The mediation of Christ is the only medium which we recognize as the means by which we approach God : and it follows that all who strive and use the means to live in Christ are united to one another in Him—" neither death, nor life " can separate them. We are content to leave in His hands all who have passed from our life here, knowing that our communion with them through Him is intensely real.

This may be fully accepted by Spiritualistic teachers and yet they might urge that such communion does not conflict with definite communication : indeed might not definite communication serve to make the fact of the spiritual world and our fellowship with it more real ? To this we should answer that the constant search for definite communication as practised by spiritualistic teachers does, in fact, arrest the development of faith, diverting us from the need and also from the means of our spiritual education to an interest in experiments to determine whether communication is possible or real and to the desire to escape from the discipline of faith. The " eye of holiness " and nothing less than holiness is required for the vision of the unseen world ; the pure in heart see God the more completely as they grow in purity. Moreover, many practices by which such communication is sought lead to a loss of true communion through the Love of God in Christ Jesus, because in them the subconscious self is released from the control of our wills, and no moral struggle for purity is made Our whole personality is not raised to the realm of spiritual being, but one element is allowed to become dominant, and that element manifestly the least regulated and regulative of our faculties, and, therefore, the most exposed to illusion and deception The Christian Scriptures undoubtedly declare the existence of unseen beings who influence men for good or evil We cannot, therefore, dismiss the possibility of communications from such beings of either nature. Such possibility will for Christians form an additional reason for precaution when they are invited to seek intercourse with the spirits of the departed We cannot insist too strongly upon the known fact that the indiscriminate and undisciplined indulgence of subconscious activity may gravely injure character, and that the habit of recourse to *séances* and " seers " leads to no spiritual benefit.

It is possible that we may be on the threshold of a new Science, which will by another method of approach confirm us in the assurance of a world behind and beyond the world we see, and of something within us by which we are in contact with it. We could never presume to set a limit to means which God may use to bring man to the realization of spiritual life. But there is nothing in the cult erected on this Science which enhances, there is, indeed, much which obscures, the meaning of that other world and our relation to it as unfolded in the Gospel of Christ and the teaching of the Church, and which depreciates the means given to us of attaining and abiding in fellowship with that world.

(b)—CHRISTIAN SCIENCE.

We desire to acknowledge the debt we owe to the Lambeth Conference of 1908 for the Report on Ministries of Healing, and to record our general agreement with that Report.

Twelve years have passed since that Report was issued. These have been years of active research and the war has provided manifold experience in all branches of healing It is therefore natural that some advance should now be made towards definite conclusions upon questions that were left open by the last Conference and that certain fundamental truths should be re-emphasized in their bearing upon present problems.

It appears to the Committee that too much emphasis has been laid in many quarters upon the distinction between what are called spiritual means of healing, and what are called physical means of healing. Wherever this distinction is wrongly made it is fatal to truth. The promise of Christ to His Church is that His Spirit shall guide His people into all the truth In view of that promise we are justified in claiming as due to the operation of the Divine Spirit all progress in the knowledge of the physical world, particularly such knowledge as is being constantly brought into the service of love through the relief of human suffering Thus we claim as due to the Spirit of the Incarnate Christ all the devoted and self-sacrificing labour in scientific research and in the application of the results of that research in medicine, surgery, nursing, hygiene and sanitation. Full account must also be taken of the great progress which has been made since the last report was issued in psychotherapeutics or psychiatry in all its branches Side by side with these we recognize that both in study and in practice there has been notable development in the direction of healing with prayer accompanied by laying-on of hands or of anointing.

In these three departments of healing considered under the heads of physical science, psychology, and religion, without making a claim to exact analysis, we seem to find some correspondence with the threefold division of Man's nature into body, mind, and spirit, and we look forward confidently to an orderly movement towards the adjustment and co-ordination of these three aspects of the work of healing.

In an age of specialized study we have constantly to be upon our guard against over emphasizing one aspect of the subject-matter. To ignore or exaggerate one aspect of healing must result in failure to achieve the full purpose of God's gifts. We believe that no one of these aspects of healing can possibly be excluded from the scope of the term spiritual. Physical means of healing can only be regarded as unspiritual when men deliberately shut their eyes to the truth that these means are the creation and gift of God. It is the task of the Church to remind and persuade all concerned in this ministry of healing, patients no less than physicians, nurses, and others, of the spiritual nature of their undertaking and to affirm our faith that in the lively sense of this lies the best hope of success.

And here we are bound with penitence to acknowledge that there has often been a grave deficiency in our Church's faith and teaching. Not sufficiently have we emphasized our Lord's revelation of the Fatherhood of God, of the fulness of His Love, of His loving care of body as well as of soul, which invites us to cast all our care upon Him.

The Gospel lesson of " God-Faith " and the inward joy and peace, of which the best Christian experience is the witness, have been allowed too often to lose their supremacy. Christians safeguard that supremacy not by ignoring or denying the fact of suffering, but by transfiguring it through the teaching, example and power of our Lord.

This neglect on our part to enforce certain aspects of the Christian faith has led inevitably to reaction. The Movement known as Christian Science for instance has undoubtedly helped to call attention to the importance of spiritual forces in the work of healing and in the promotion of happiness and general well-being. This movement has, however, tended, often with grave results both to children and to adults, to disparage all physical methods of healing and God's gift of scientific research and knowledge which is intended to be received and used with thanksgiving.

Under the influence of this pseudo-spirituality Christian Science has developed doctrines which, so far as we can gather from its text-book, appear to be in direct conflict with the Christian faith. We need only dwell upon one or two of these points.

(1) Christian Science emphasizes the Oneness of God and of the Universe in a way that does not in fact escape from pantheism. Oneness is regarded as undifferentiated Oneness in which no real place is left for distinctions or for variety. Personal terms are used of God but are at the same time declared to be synonymous with impersonal Principle. As against this we would urge the fulness of the teaching of the Catholic Faith concerning the Personal Being of God as revealed in the doctrines of the Incarnation and of the Blessed Trinity.

(2) Christian Science in fact revives the old dualism of matter and Spirit : matter is wholly illusory, the source of nothing but error and therefore evil As against this the Catholic Faith teaches that while Spirit is supreme, matter is a vehicle through which Spirit finds expression : the whole world is sacramental : we touch here a conviction that is fundamental to the Christian faith. If matter, as Christian Science maintains, is non-existent and cannot enter into the consciousness of God, the Incarnation of the Son of God in human nature is impossible, and Scriptural teaching upon the redemption of man and of creation becomes meaningless.

(3) In the presentation of our Lord a distinction is made between Christ the ideal Truth and Jesus the human prophet of Galilee. Jesus becomes the man who more than any other man proved the Principle which heals the sick and casts out error to be divine There is no essential distinction between our Saviour and all other men—though a difference in the degree of possession of the Christ Ideal is fully emphasized There is no conception at all of grace coming to men through Jesus Christ ; we are only invited to follow in His steps as of one who is the Wayshower.

(4) The denial of the reality of sin empties the Atonement of its usual Christian content.

In the light of what has been said we would urge the following practical recommendations :—
There should be—

(1) Clearer and more constant teaching as well as study of the full doctrine of the Church in its bearing upon true spirituality.

(2) Teaching about Prayer and Holy Communion ; special efficacy is promised to the " prayer of faith " ; this prayer may be offered by individuals, by congregations in Church, and by prayer-circles formed of those who desire to forward the work of healing. In Holy Communion also the thought of our Saviour's care of the body has its place ; in the words of administration the preservation of the body is mentioned side by side with the preservation of the soul.

(3) We would urge the recognition of the Ministry and gifts of healing in the Church, and that these should be exercised under due licence and authority.

This, in our opinion, will involve :—

(a) Instruction both of clergy and laity so that the corporate faith of the Church may be stimulated and the power to heal may be released.

(b) Training : we feel that it is important that Candidates for Holy Orders should be equipped by training in psychology, and be given some acquaintance with methods and principles of healing. Only so will the clergy be enabled rightly to direct the thought of their people on the subject and to discriminate between truth and error

(c) Revision of the Office of the Visitation of the Sick , or the provision under due authority from National or Provincial Churches, of an alternative office containing recommendations and regulations for laying-on of hands with prayer for recovery with or without unction as may be desired.

(d) Authorization : all who are licensed under due authority for this work should be persons who are loyal to the Church's Faith and Sacraments, who are willing to work in full co-operation with the Medical profession, and who are willing to work also in loyal co-operation with the parochial clergy.

In conclusion, while unable to dwell upon the many problems which the whole subject raises, relating to the mystery of pain and suffering, we may say that while disease is a part of the lack of harmony with the perfect will of God, and thus that all healing powers are an expression of God's will and power to heal, yet pain and suffering in themselves also bear witness to the working of God's laws in nature in this present order The ordeal of life here is the education of the human spirit in full obedience to God and trust in Him ; suffering, therefore, may be overruled by God for blessing, and is, within our experience, constantly so over-ruled, becoming thus a means of true spiritual growth and of intimate fellowship with our Saviour. " Who learned obedience by the things which He suffered ; and being made perfect, became the author of eternal salvation unto all them that obey Him."

(c)—THEOSOPHY.

The Theosophical Society represents a vigorous revival of earlier mystical and occult philosophies. The rediscovery of the teaching of Asiatic religions, the realization of latent psychical powers in human nature, the revolt against exclusivism and traditionalism in some current forms of Christian theology, the recognition of the continuity and unity of human evolution, all these factors combined to create a demand for a more complete

synthesis of all human knowledge and belief   Modern Theosophy
offers to supply this demand.   It is however extremely difficult
to determine what Theosophy is.   Representative English
theosophists insist that the Theosophical Society stands only
for its three stated objects, *viz.* (1) " to form a nucleus of the
Universal Brotherhood of Humanity without distinction of race,
creed, sex, caste or colour," (2) " to encourage the study of
comparative religion, philosophy and science," (3) " to investigate
the unexplained laws of nature and the powers latent in man "
The Society disclaims any authoritative or obligatory body of
teaching or any official identification with the views propounded
by its leaders.   It consists of " students belonging to any
religion in the world or to none," and " their bond of union is
not the profession of a common belief but a common search
and aspiration for Truth."   Your Committee, while accepting
these statements, cannot but regard the Theosophical Society
as incurring a certain measure of responsibility by the publication
and circulation of theosophical literature.   In a booklet entitled
" Theosophy and the Mission of the Theosophical Society,"
published by the Society and lately sent to members of the
Lambeth Conference, it is stated that " Theosophy is the body
of truths which forms the basis of all religions and which cannot
be claimed as the exclusive possession of any."   " The immanence
of God, the solidarity of man, such are the basic truths of
Theosophy."   " Its secondary teachings are those which are
the common teachings of all religions, living or dead."   Among
these are reincarnation, karma, and " the existence of divine
Teachers, superhuman Men, often called the White Brotherhood "   And " it is the mission of the Theosophical Society as
a whole to spread these truths in every land."   Your committee
desire to point out that the literature of the Society contains a
large amount of common positive teaching embodying a definite
and distinctive view of the universe, which we are therefore
justified in regarding and describing in this report under the
title of Theosophy.

The Committee recognize frankly that there is nothing in
the Christian faith which precludes sympathy with the pursuit
of the three stated objects of the Theosophical Society.   The
methods and alleged results of theosophical study are quite
another question.   Theosophical leaders and teachers claim to
impart knowledge derived from occult sources.   They claim to
be in communication with a brotherhood of pioneers of the
human race who have reached the goal of their own evolution
and now control and guide the evolution of their race by operations in the unseen world or by reincarnation on earth.   They
claim also that they have themselves by a process of mystical
self-discipline developed latent powers of consciousness which
enable them to read occult traces left in the etheric records of

the universe by past events and experiences. We regret that the occult methods of theosophists are not made available for scientific investigation, especially in view of the fact that their theory of different organs and planes of human consciousness, for example, is stated to be " a matter not of speculation but of observation and experiment." The Christian Church has nothing to fear from established conclusions of sound psychical research, for the Christian faith is not identified with or dependent on any particular theory of the constituents of human consciousness. But we cannot resist the impression that the methods of theosophical occultism are not free from psychical conditions of a morbid and demoralizing tendency. The secrecy of an esoteric section pledged not to reveal its methods and experience is in any case not a healthy atmosphere for the search after divine truth.

The theosophical conception of God is too elusive for precise analysis. In the West it appears to be a nebulous theism, but significantly enough in India it assumes somewhat of a pantheistic or even polytheistic form. Everywhere it tends to exaggerate the affinity between human and divine spirit into identity, and its real inwardness is evident in the theosophical presentation of Christ. It is in the twin doctrines of reincarnation and karma that Theosophy begins to come into more or less direct conflict with the Christian faith. The doctrine of reincarnation appears to us both philosophically and scientifically unsound. But our concern is rather to insist that this doctrine, which theosophists preach as a lost element of true Christianity, can only be found in the New Testament by an arbitrary and artificial exegesis ; that in its theoretical explanation it leaves apparently no place for conscious continuity of personality or of personal relationships ; that in its practical working it tends to destroy both perseverance and sympathy. The doctrine of karma or the law of consequence, namely, that the quantitative karma or result of a man's conduct must be worked off gradually in this or some future existence, evacuates forgiveness of all spiritual reality. A doctrine which drives its exponents to describe Christ's absolution of the penitent as a mere announcement that his karma was exhausted is the very negation of any conception of divine forgiveness.

The conflict between Theosophy and the Christian faith becomes irreconcilable when we reach the central fact of Christianity, the Person of Christ. Theosophy teaches that " the Jesus Christ of the Churches " is a fusion of three distinct elements—historical, mythical and mystical. " The historical Christ is a glorious being belonging to the great spiritual hierarchy that guides the spiritual evolution of humanity, who used for three years the human body of the disciple Jesus." This Jesus was a Jew born 105 B.C. and trained in the occult lore of the

East in Egyptian and Essene brotherhoods until the time came for him to lend his body for the incarnation of a supreme Teacher. Afterwards, while the Christ " visited His disciples for something over fifty years in His subtle spiritual body . . . training them in a knowledge of occult truths," the man Jesus " perfected his human evolution " and " became the Lord and Master of the Church founded by the Christ." At the present time Jesus, " clothed in a body he has taken from Syria, is waiting the time for his reappearance in the open life of men." Meanwhile he " lives mostly in the mountains of Lebanon." Instead of the one Jesus Christ, God and man, we are here given two persons : a Christ who is divine but not God, and a Jesus promoted from humanity to quasi-divinity.

" The mythical Christ " means that the cardinal facts embodied in Christian creeds and holy days were not historical facts but myths attached to " the Christ of the Church " as they had been attached to similar beings in earlier religions. " The mystical Christ " is the truth symbolized by the myth. The Christ-myth represents the descent of the divine Word into matter in creation, and the birth and ascent of the human Christ. This indwelling Christ is the higher self of man, a self-evolution of the higher nature of man, typified by the gospel allegory but independent of any historical Christ. It is sufficient here to point out that this triple Christ of theosophical research, presented to us on the authority of " the occult records " is not the Christ of the New Testament. It is a flagrant contradiction of the Gospels. It is a subtler but no less radical contradiction of the Christian mysticism of St. Paul, for whom the Christ-life in man is always dependent upon the reality both of the redemption wrought by the Incarnation and of the present activity of the ascended Christ.

The uniqueness of the Person of Christ involves the universality of His mission and message. Theosophy in denying the uniqueness of the Person of Christ denies the universality of the Christian religion. It teaches that beneath the exoteric form of all religions there lay and still lies the same esoteric body of essential truths—that the Christianity of the Churches is only the exoteric form of the Christian religion—and that the mission of Theosophy is to reveal and restore the lost esoteric truths of this and every religion. Theosophy therefore consistently discounts and discourages the missionary claim of Christianity, for it denies that Christianity has anything essential to give which is not already contained in the esoteric truths of other religions. Theosophy here represents the extreme recoil of modern thought from the older view which saw little or no truth in non-Christian religions. That view is foreign to the Christian faith and has long ceased to dominate Christian missionary thought. The Christian Church stands for the belief

that truth and life in religion everywhere come through the Word
working in the world, and that what all races and peoples need
now is the fuller life and truth which can only come from conscious
knowledge of the Word made flesh, the historical Christ who
was and is the Son of God.

The Committee, while acknowledging that there is nothing
in the avowed objects of the Theosophical Society which is in
itself incompatible with loyal membership of the Church, desire
to impress urgently upon the members of the Church the necessity
of the greatest caution in pursuing the study of Theosophy.
Theosophists use the language of Christian adoration but in
senses which are not those of the Christian faith ; and their
language is so Christian in sound that their disciples fail to realize
how far they are being carried away from the Christian position.
We urge Christian people therefore to examine very carefully
every stage of the teaching offered them in the name of Theosophy.
The need of such examination is already evident in the case of
theosophical teaching with regard to Jesus Christ. It is seen
vividly too in the case of the Order of the Star in the East, an
Order founded in India in 1911 " to draw together those who
whether inside or outside the Theosophical Society believe in
the near coming of a great Spiritual Teacher for the helping
of the world." The stated principles of the Order contain
much that is in harmony with Christian self-discipline. But
we feel bound to warn Church people against allowing themselves
to be drawn unthinkingly into the Order by their expectation
of the coming of Christ. The current expositions of the work
of the coming Teacher appear to us to ignore the teaching
mission of the Holy Spirit, and in other ways also to misinterpret
the New Testament, which represents the future Advent of
Christ not as a second ministry of sowing but as a harvest of
results—not as a new gospel but as a judgement. But there is
a far graver danger in the fact that the Order in India, its birth-
place and headquarters, is associated with positive teaching to
the effect that the coming Christ is identical with the Lord
Maitreya of Buddhist mythology, and is to be incarnate in the
body of a Tamil youth now living, named Krishnamurti. We
urge Church people attracted by the apparently or potentially
Christian character and outlook of the Order to consider seriously
whether they can reconcile this teaching with their own faith
in Christ.

Secondly, we urge Christian people to remember that in
view of the fact that most students of Theosophy are necessarily
dependent upon the teaching and guidance of a few members
of the esoteric section, it is of vital importance to examine the
character and credentials of the exponents of Theosophy upon
whose authority they are encouraged almost blindly to rely.
We urge them to bear constantly in mind St. John's warning

K

to Christians beset by an earlier stage of Theosophy—" Believe not every spirit, but try the spirits whether they are of God."

The Committee desire to close their report with a positive note of recommendation. The attraction of Theosophy for many thoughtful Christian minds lies largely in its presentation of Christian faith and life as a quest. Christian faith is indeed a quest for truth yet to be revealed no less than a grasp of truth already revealed. The pastoral care of the Church for the common needs of all souls requires simple and definite doctrinal statement, such as the Church has always provided. At the same time we must admit that different schools of thought within the Church are alike in danger of falling into a stereo-typed line of teaching, into a narrow dogmatism and traditional-ism forgetful of the needs of such souls as are deeply conscious of the mystery into which all known truths shade off and of the fascinating and perplexing questions on which Bible and Creed alike leave speculation free. Responsible teachers of the Church therefore—and the clergy are called to be teachers no less than preachers—will do well to remember both of the lines on which the great early Christian teachers met and answered gnostic theosophy of their day. Like Tertullian and Irenaeus we must insist on the plain meaning of Scripture and the unity and continuity of traditional Christian belief. But also like Clement and Origen we may claim all life and learning as food for Christian thought, developing what might be called a true Christian theosophy, embracing the spiritual experiences of poets, saints and mystics, and reverently speculating beyond the borders of revelation, so long as we hold fast to the historic facts of the Creed and to the sacramental communion of the Church

The Committee, while pleading for a larger place to be given in the teaching of the Church to the mystical elements of faith and life, desire earnestly to advise all thinking people to safe-guard their Christian position by making the fullest study and use of the treasures of knowledge and thought to be found in Bible, Creed and Sacrament as they have been interpreted by sound Christian scholarship and philosophy. The Committee in this connexion welcome the forward movement of the Society for the Promotion of Christian Knowledge in the way of pro-viding Christian literature of the first rank, and commend the efforts made by various agencies and associations within the Church for the higher religious education of the faithful laity.

(Signed)   HUBERT M. OXON:
Chairman.

REPORT OF THE COMMITTEE † APPOINTED TO CONSIDER RELATION
TO AND REUNION WITH OTHER CHURCHES—(*a*) EPISCOPAL
CHURCHES, (*b*) NON-EPISCOPAL CHURCHES, WITH QUESTIONS
AS TO (i) RECOGNITION OF MINISTERS; (ii) " VALIDITY " OF
SACRAMENTS, (iii) SUGGESTED TRANSITIONAL STEPS

THE Committee appointed to consider and report upon
relation to and reunion with other Churches divided itself into
two sub-committees dealing with the two main divisions of the
subject submitted for their consideration, namely (*a*) Episcopal
Churches, and (*b*) Non-Episcopal Churches Of these two
sub-committees, the former was presided over by the Bishop of
Gloucester, and the second by the chairman of the whole Committee

The whole Committee is responsible for the first part of
the Report, including the Appeal, and Resolutions which follow
this part. Each Sub-Committee is responsible for its own
Report and for the Resolutions founded upon it.

† Names of Members of the Committee ·—

Bishop of Aberdeen
Archbishop of Algoma
Bishop of Argyll (*a*)
Archbishop of Armagh
Bishop of Atlanta
Bishop of Bath and Wells*
Bishop Hamilton Baynes
Bishop of Bethlehem
Bishop of Bombay (*Secretary*)
Bishop of Brechin (Primus)
Archbishop of Brisbane
Bishop of Bristol (*Secretary*)
Bishop of Chelmsford
Bishop of Chichester
Bishop of Columbia
Bishop of Derby
Bishop of Derry
Bishop of Dornakal
Bishop of Down
Bishop Du Moulin (Ohio Coadjutor)
Bishop of Durham
Bishop of Ely
Bishop of Gibraltar (*a*)
Bishop of Gloucester (*a*)

Bishop of Hankow
Bishop of Harrisburg (*a*)
Bishop in Jerusalem (*a*) (*Secretary*)
Bishop Johnson (Missouri Coadjutor)
Bishop Joscelyne
Bishop in Khartoum (*a*)
Bishop King (*a*)
Bishop of Kootenay
Bishop of Kyushu
Bishop of Madras
Bishop of Manchester
Bishop of Massachusetts
Bishop of Meath
Archbishop of Melbourne
Bishop of Mombasa
Bishop of Montreal
Bishop of Moray and Ross (*a*)
Bishop of Nassau
Bishop of Norwich
Bishop of Olympia
Bishop of Ontario
Bishop of Pennsylvania
Bishop of Peterborough
Bishop of Pretoria

(*a*) Members of Sub-Committee on Episcopal Churches   The remainder
formed the Sub-Committee on Non-Episcopal Churches.

K 2

Part I.

Report of the Whole Committee.

The reunion of the separated congregations of Christ's flock is fundamental to all the subjects dealt with by the Lambeth Conference. For the manifold witness of the Church would be intensified and extended beyond all measure if it came from an undivided Society of Jesus Christ. To restore the unity of this Society, therefore, would be to increase the effective force of this witness in every part of the world to a degree which in these days can be scarcely imagined. No one who is not blind to the signs which abound on every hand can doubt that the Spirit of God is moving in this direction in a way which must bring home to the authorities of all Christian Communions a deep sense of responsibility in the face of an opportunity which is almost without parallel in the history of the Church. It was with a full, and indeed an overwhelming, sense of this responsibility that the members of this Committee entered upon the task committed to it. In spite of the differences of opinion which we brought with us to the consideration of our subject we seemed to be guided towards an ideal of Christian unity which we have endeavoured to express in the Appeal which we place in the forefront of our resolutions. It appeared to us that we could best fulfil the duty laid upon us at this present time by placing this ideal before all who love our Lord Jesus Christ in sincerity, in the hope that, if it be in accordance with God's will, it may by His blessing serve to inspire and guide a new and united movement towards the fulfilment of His purpose for the unity of His Church.

Names of Members of the Committee—*continued*.

Archbishop of Rupert's Land	Bishop in Tinnevelly
Bishop of St Albans	Bishop of Truro (a) (*Secretary*)
Bishop of St Andrews	Bishop of Uganda
Bishop of St David's	Bishop of Waiapu
Bishop of St. John's (a)	Bishop of Warrington
Bishop of Salisbury	Bishop of Western New York
Bishop of Southern Brazil	Bishop of Willesden (a)
Bishop of South Carolina	Bishop Mott Williams* (a)
Bishop of Southern Ohio (a)	Bishop of Willochra
Bishop in South Tokyo	Bishop of Winchester
Archbishop of Sydney	Archbishop of York (*Chairman*)
Bishop of Tennessee	Bishop of Zanzibar

(a) Members of Sub-Committee on Episcopal Churches. The remainder formed the Sub-Committee on Non-Episcopal Churches.

We therefore venture to recommend that the Conference should adopt and send forth the following Appeal to all Christian people.

AN APPEAL TO ALL CHRISTIAN PEOPLE

FROM THE BISHOPS ASSEMBLED IN THE LAMBETH CONFERENCE OF 1920.

We, Archbishops, Bishops Metropolitan, and other Bishops of the Holy Catholic Church in full communion with the Church of England, in Conference assembled, realizing the responsibility which rests upon us at this time, and sensible of the sympathy and the prayers of many, both within and without our own Communion, make this appeal to all Christian people

We acknowledge all those who believe in our Lord Jesus Christ, and have been baptized into the name of the Holy Trinity, as sharing with us membership in the universal Church of Christ which is His Body. We believe that the Holy Spirit has called us in a very solemn and special manner to associate ourselves in penitence and prayer with all those who deplore the divisions of Christian people, and are inspired by the vision and hope of a visible unity of the whole Church.

I We believe that God wills fellowship. By God's own act this fellowship was made in and through Jesus Christ, and its life is in His Spirit We believe that it is God's purpose to manifest this fellowship, so far as this world is concerned, in an outward, visible, and united society, holding one faith, having its own recognized officers, using God-given means of grace, and inspiring all its members to the world-wide service of the Kingdom of God This is what we mean by the Catholic Church

II This united fellowship is not visible in the world to-day. On the one hand there are other ancient episcopal Communions in East and West, to whom ours is bound by many ties of common faith and tradition On the other hand there are the great non-episcopal Communions, standing for rich elements of truth, liberty and life which might otherwise have been obscured or neglected With them we are closely linked by many affinities— racial, historical and spiritual We cherish the earnest hope that all these Communions, and our own, may be led by the Spirit into the unity of the Faith and of the knowledge of the Son of God. But in fact we are all organized in different groups, each one keeping to itself gifts that rightly belong to the whole fellowship, and tending to live its own life apart from the rest.

III. The causes of division lie deep in the past, and are by no means simple or wholly blameworthy. Yet none can doubt that self-will, ambition, and lack of charity among Christians have been principal factors in the mingled process, and that these, together with blindness to the sin of disunion, are still mainly responsible for the breaches of Christendom We acknowledge this condition of broken fellowship to be contrary to God's will, and we desire frankly to confess our share in the guilt of thus crippling the Body of Christ and hindering the activity of His Spirit.

IV. The times call us to a new outlook and new measures. The Faith cannot be adequately apprehended and the battle of the Kingdom cannot be worthily fought while the body is divided, and is thus unable to grow up into the fulness of the life of Christ The time has come, we believe, for all the separated groups of Christians to agree in forgetting the things which are behind and reaching out towards the goal of a reunited Catholic Church The removal of the barriers which have arisen between them will only be brought about by a new comradeship of those whose faces are definitely set this way.

The vision which rises before us is that of a Church, genuinely Catholic, loyal to all Truth, and gathering into its fellowship all "who profess and call themselves Christians," within whose visible unity all the treasures of faith and order, bequeathed as a heritage by the past to the present, shall be possessed in common, and made serviceable to the whole body of Christ. Within this unity Christian Communions now separated from one another would retain much that has long been distinctive in their methods of worship and service. It is through a rich diversity of life and devotion that the unity of the whole fellowship will be fulfilled.

V. This means an adventure of goodwill and still more of faith, for nothing less is required than a new discovery of the creative resources of God. To this adventure we are convinced that God is now calling all the members of His Church.

VI We believe that the visible unity of the Church will be found to involve the whole-hearted acceptance of :—

The Holy Scriptures, as the record of God's revelation of Himself to man, and as being the rule and ultimate standard of faith ; and the Creed commonly called Nicene, as the sufficient statement of the Christian faith, and either it or the Apostles' Creed as the Baptismal confession of belief :

The divinely instituted sacraments of Baptism and the Holy Communion, as expressing for all the corporate life of the whole fellowship in and with Christ :

A ministry acknowledged by every part of the Church as possessing not only the inward call of the Spirit, but also the commission of Christ and the authority of the whole body.

VII. May we not reasonably claim that the Episcopate is the one means of providing such a ministry ? It is not that we call in question for a moment the spiritual reality of the ministries of those Communions which do not possess the Episcopate. On the contrary we thankfully acknowledge that these ministries have been manifestly blessed and owned by the Holy Spirit as effective means of grace. But we submit that considerations alike of history and of present experience justify the claim which we make on behalf of the Episcopate. Moreover, we would urge that it is now and will prove to be in the future the best instrument for maintaining the unity and continuity of the Church. But we greatly desire that the office of a Bishop should be everywhere exercised in a representative and constitutional manner, and more truly express all that ought to be involved for the life of the Christian Family in the title of Father-in-God. Nay more, we eagerly look forward to the day when through its acceptance in a united Church we may all share in that grace which is pledged to the members of the whole body in the apostolic rite of the laying-on of hands, and in the joy and fellowship of a Eucharist in which as one Family we may together, without any doubtfulness of mind, offer to the one Lord our worship and service.

VIII. We believe that for all the truly equitable approach to union is by the way of mutual deference to one another's consciences To this end, we who send forth this appeal would say that if the authorities of other Communions should so desire, we are persuaded that, terms of union having been otherwise satisfactorily adjusted, Bishops and clergy of our Communion would willingly accept from these authorities a form of commission or recognition which would commend our ministry to their congregations, as having its place in the one family life. It is not in our power to know how far this suggestion may be acceptable to those to whom we offer it. We can only say that we offer it in all sincerity as a token of our longing that all ministries of grace, theirs and ours, shall be available for the service of our Lord in a united Church.

It is our hope that the same motive would lead ministers who have not received it to accept a commission through episcopal ordination, as obtaining for them a ministry throughout the whole fellowship.

In so acting no one of us could possibly be taken to repudiate his past ministry God forbid that any man should repudiate a past experience rich in spiritual blessings for himself and others. Nor would any of us be dishonouring the Holy Spirit of God, Whose call led us all to our several ministries, and Whose power enabled us to perform them We shall be publicly and formally seeking additional recognition of a new call to wider service in a reunited Church, and imploring for ourselves God's grace and strength to fulfil the same.

IX. The spiritual leadership of the Catholic Church in days to come, for which the world is manifestly waiting, depends upon the readiness with which each group is prepared to make sacrifices for the sake of a common fellowship, a common ministry, and a common service to the world.

We place this ideal first and foremost before ourselves and our own people. We call upon them to make the effort to meet the demands of a new age with a new outlook. To all other Christian people whom our words may reach we make the same appeal. We do not ask that any one Communion should consent to be absorbed in another. We do ask them to unite with us in a new and great endeavour to recover and to manifest to the world the unity of the Body of Christ for which He prayed.

The Lambeth Conference of 1908 passed the following resolution (No. 78) " The constituted authorities of the various Churches of the Anglican Communion should, as opportunity offers, arrange conferences with representatives of other Christian Churches, and meetings for common acknowledgement of the sins of division, and for intercession for the growth of unity."

In another part of this Report it is shewn that in many countries, particularly in the United States of America, in India, and in Africa, this course has been very largely followed But the urgency of the present world situation, and the wide and deep longing for unity which these Conferences have revealed, and which fills the hearts of Christian people throughout the world, seem to us to call for further and more responsible action. We ask the Conference to recommend that the authorities of the Churches of the Anglican Communion should, in such ways and at such times as they think best, formally invite the authorities of other Churches within their areas to confer with them as to the posssibility of taking definite steps to co-operate in a common endeavour, on the lines set forth in the Appeal, to restore the unity of the Church of Christ. It may be that these approaches will meet with some rebuffs and disappointments Special circumstances may be urged as shewing that such conferences would be premature. Some doors seem for the present to be shut. But many doors in all parts of the world are open There are already movements in progress for a closer union of Communions separated from us and from one another. With the spirit and hopes of these movements we would associate ourselves, heartily desiring their success and trusting that they may forward the cause of the ultimate union of the universal Church Yet the historical traditions and the spiritual sympathies of the Anglican Church seem to lay upon us a special duty, which at this present time we ought to accept as a definite call of God. May He in His mercy forgive and take from us any spirit of self-satisfaction ! We have need frankly to acknowledge and humbly to confess our manifold sins and shortcomings as a Church In all our approaches to our fellow Christians of other Churches we shall try to make it plain that we only desire to be permitted to take our part with them in a cause to which the Lord Whom we serve is at this time most manifestly calling all the members of His Church.

Here it will not be out of place to draw the attention of our fellow-churchmen to some important results of the extension and development of the Anglican Communion, and the bearing of these upon the question of reunion and upon our attitude and duty towards it

At the date of the first Lambeth Conference, 1867, this Communion had taken the form of a federation of self-governing Churches, held together for the most part without legal sanctions by a common reverence for the same traditions and a common use of a Prayer Book which, in spite of some local variations, was virtually the same. Our missionary workers were then planting churches among nations very different from the Anglo-Saxon race and from one another, but as yet these had shewn but little growth. In the interval between that time and the present there have grown up indigenous Churches in China, in Japan, in East and West Africa, in each of which the English members are but a handful of strangers and sojourners, some engaged in missionary work, some in secular business. In India the Church includes large numbers both of British and of Indian members : the emergence of a National Church, claiming freedom to regulate its own affairs, is only a matter of time. Consequently the Anglican Communion of to-day is a federation of Churches, some national, some regional, but no longer predominantly Anglo-Saxon in race, nor can it be expected that it will attach special value to Anglo-Saxon traditions. The blessing which has rested upon its work has brought it to a new point of view. Meanwhile, it might also be said that its centre of gravity is shifting. It already presents an example on a small scale of the problems which attach to the unity of a Universal Church. As the years go on, its ideals must become less Anglican and more Catholic. It cannot look to any bonds of union holding it together, other than those which should hold together the Catholic Church itself

While this development has been going on, another has kept pace with it. Our Communion has taken into itself, tried, and found valuable many elements which were not to be found in any effective condition in the Church of England one hundred or even fifty years ago. The bearing of these on the problem of reunion is so important that we deem it worth while to notice here some examples. In most parts of our Communion the Episcopate does not even present the appearance of autocracy or prelacy. Various arrangements have been adopted by which the Bishop is elected by the Diocese over which he is to preside. The affairs of the Diocese are managed by the Bishop in conjunction with a Diocesan Synod or Council. The Bishops and their Dioceses are further correlated in Provincial and General Synods, Conventions or Assemblies. Thus, Episcopacy among us has generally become constitutional, and the clergy and laity have attained to a share in the government of the Church. Again, in many parts of our Communion systems of patronage have been adopted which recognize the right of congregations to take part in the selection of their ministers. We draw attention to these matters as evidencing our recognition, not only in word but in deed, of the value of some of those elements of Church life which those now separated from us have developed with marked success. We would urge further on our own fellow-churchmen that it is one of the most pressing and most important steps towards reunion that they should develop in every place, according to its own circumstances and the genius of its people, the well-tried principles of constitutionalism in the government of the Church, and of the full employment of every member in its life, and the Committee venture to submit a Resolution to this effect to the Conference.

There are other signs of similar expansion from within, which have made our Communion more representative of the varying phases of Christian life and devotion. The development of mission services and missions of many kinds, the use of various additional forms of prayer, of *ex tempore* prayer, of silent prayer, and again of various kinds of ceremonial and elaboration of liturgical worship, testify, quite apart from the merits of any of them, to the increasing recognition of the diversity of the temperaments of men and of the duty of the Church to make them all feel at home in the family of God. We welcome the spirit of that expansion which has brought one part or another of our Communion nearer to those who are separated from us. We look forward hopefully to the far greater variety in the expression of the one faith and of devotion to the one Lord, which must necessarily ensue when the Churches of men who are strangers in blood, though brothers in Christ, come to fuller age and to more characteristic development. We call upon our fellow-churchmen in every branch of our Communion to accept ever more fully the standard of the universal Church and its necessary inclusiveness, so that they will not feel strange when they are called upon to live in the fellowship of the re-united universal Church.

Meanwhile, the needs of the whole world lay upon Christian men and women everywhere the obligation to manifest the fellowship which they already possess as believers in the one Lord, and as the soldiers and servants of His Kingdom, by praying and working together for the vindication of the Christian Faith and the extension of the rule of Christ among all nations and over every region of human life. We therefore recommend that,

where it has not already been done, Councils representing all
Christian Communions should be formed within such areas as may
be deemed most convenient, as centres of united effort to promote
the physical, moral and social welfare of the people and the spread
of the Kingdom of God and of His righteousness among men.
Such co-operation will, we are confident, both strengthen the desire
and prepare the way for a fuller spiritual union of life and worship.

Part II

Report of the Sub-Committee (*b*) on Relation to and Reunion with Non-Episcopal Churches.

[Note.—*In view of the fact that the report of Sub-Committee (b)
on Non-Episcopal Churches is specially based upon the Appeal to
all Christian People, and repeatedly refers to it, it is here placed
before the report of Sub-Committee (a) on Episcopal Churches*]

We first pass in review the movements towards reunion in which
the Anglican Churches have recently been involved.

The character of the movement towards reunion with non-
episcopal Churches since the last Lambeth Conference has been
dramatic and impressive   This is notably true of the movement
in the American Church in 1910, resulting in the proposals for
a World Conference on Questions of Faith and Order, which
shall represent all Christians and which has already secured the
interest and co-operation of many Christian bodies throughout
the world   Further, in almost every section of the Anglican
Communion conferences with other Churches have been held,
in not a few cases definite proposals have been made, and in
others actual schemes set forth   Of this we have received
striking illustrations. They range from simple conferences
where differences have been discussed and lines of agreement
indicated, to definite proposals where substantial agreement
has been obtained.   In the first category are to be found the
important first and second Interim Reports of the English Joint
Sub-Committee appointed in connexion with the World Conference
on Faith and Order, to which our Appeal, as set forth above,
is greatly indebted   In addition to these, conferences between
leading members of our Church and leaders of non-episcopal
Churches have been held at Oxford and elsewhere , by chaplains
and Y.M.C A. workers in France ; and by the Bishop of London
with members of the Wesleyan Church , while the Convocations
of both Canterbury and York have had under consideration
certain proposals relating to united fellowship and worship.

All these witness to the deep and earnest longing in the hearts of all Christian men to draw nearer to each other, and, if possible, to find some solution of the difficulties which now stand in the way of visible union. Moreover, they all reveal a far greater measure of agreement, as to both faith and order, than is generally supposed to exist.

It is, however, in the more defined and official proposals for union that we perceive how great is the progress which has been attained.

Of these proposals the following have been specially brought before us for consideration

In the United States of America a Concordat has been proposed by members of the Protestant Episcopal Church and Ministers of Congregational Churches. These proposals were presented to the General Convention of the Protestant Episcopal Church at Detroit in October, 1919. A series of resolutions was concurred in by both the House of Deputies and the House of Bishops, and a proposed canon has been drawn up The whole matter is to be considered at the next General Convention which meets in 1922.

In South India a proposed union of the Anglican Church with the South India United Church (which includes five separate non-episcopal missions) has reached a stage at which the proposals may shortly be brought before the Episcopal Synod of the Province of India and Ceylon

In East Africa a Constitution of an Alliance of Missionary Societies has been adopted, and the Members of the Alliance declare that they " pledge themselves not to rest until they can all share one Ministry."

In Australia proposals, having as their object a union with the Presbyterians, have been under consideration, and several conferences have been held with representatives of other non-Episcopal churches Much will depend upon the decisions of this Conference as to the possibility of further progress in this region

We have also received communications from Canada and China indicating the earnest desire of the Churches in both these parts of the world that definite steps in the cause of reunion may be taken

The information which we have thus briefly summarized shews most impressively the strength of the tide which is everywhere setting towards a new Christian fellowship, but with equal impressiveness it shews the widely differing problems which the Churches of the Anglican Communion throughout the world are called to face: The conditions of national and religious life in regions so diverse as, for example, India, China, East Africa, Australia, the United States of America, Canada, Scotland and England, are obviously wholly different There must be a corresponding variety in the ways along which union among

Christian people in these countries can be either approached or carried through. We therefore unanimously submit to the Conference the two following Resolutions :—

That this Conference desires to express its profound thankfulness for the important movements towards Unity, which during the last twelve years have taken place in many parts of the world, and for the earnest desire for Reunion which has been manifested both in our own Communion and among the Churches now separated from us.

That this Conference confidently commits to the various authorities of the Churches within the Anglican Communion the task of effecting union with other Christian Communions on lines that are in general harmony with the principles underlying its proposals and resolutions

We cannot insist too strongly that the resolutions which we now submit must be read and understood in the light of the ideal and principles of union which are set forth in the appeal which we have asked the Conference to issue. Taken by themselves they would inevitably misrepresent the warmth of desire and strength of hope by which we are animated They must be regarded as counsels which the Conference may rightly be expected to give to the authorities of Churches in the Anglican Communion who desire to be guided aright in their efforts to set forward the cause of Christian Unity.

We consider that when men set their faces steadily towards the ideal of our appeal, and specially when negotiations for organic reunion are in progress or again when a scheme of union has in any place been adopted, situations will arise in which we should all agree that new lines of action may be followed. In regard to such situations, we submit to the Conference the following Resolutions :—

That a Bishop is justified in giving occasional authorization to ministers, not episcopally ordained, who in his judgement are working towards an ideal of union such as is described in our Appeal, to preach in churches within his Diocese, and to clergy of the Diocese to preach in the churches of such ministers

That Bishops of the Anglican Communion will not question the action of any Bishop who, in the few years during which a definite scheme of union is maturing, shall countenance the irregularity of admitting to Communion the baptized but unconfirmed Communicants of the non-episcopal congregations concerned in the scheme.

Further, we deem it necessary in order that negotiations for union shall be steps towards and not away from our ideal, to express our dissent from certain proposals which have been, or might be, made, and which seem to us likely to obscure our ideal

or to hinder its fulfilment. Moreover, we deprecate such proposals as likely to prevent the members of our own Communion
from forwarding the work of reunion with that enthusiastic
unanimity with which it ought to be pursued. In these con-
nexions we submit to the Conference the following Resolutions :—

That this Conference cannot approve of general schemes of
intercommunion or exchange of pulpits

That in accordance with the principle of Church order set forth
in the Preface to the Ordinal attached to the Book of Common
Prayer the Conference cannot approve the Celebration in Anglican
churches of the Holy Communion for members of the Anglican
Church by ministers who have not been episcopally ordained,
and declares that the same principle requires that it should
be regarded as the general rule of the Church that Anglican
communicants should receive Holy Communion only at the hands
of ministers of their own Church, or of Churches in communion
therewith.

The general subject of the admission to Holy Communion of
persons who do not belong to any Church in communion with us
has been confused by certain doubts and varieties of practice on
which we deem it desirable that this Conference should express
its opinion. In this regard we submit to the Conference the
following Resolutions which we believe to be applicable at all
times, and not only in view of the approach of reunion :—

That no priest has canonical authority to refuse Communion
to any baptized person kneeling before the Lord's Table, unless
he be excommunicate by name, or, in the canonical sense of
the term, a cause of scandal to the faithful.

Nothing in these Resolutions is intended to indicate that the
rule of Confirmation as conditioning admission to the Holy
Communion must necessarily apply to the case of baptized persons
who seek Communion under conditions which in the Bishop's
judgement justify their admission thereto.

It is plainly impossible to draft Resolutions which would
meet every case that might arise anywhere in the course of
negotiations for union or to suggest terms of union to meet every
contingency. Great freedom must be left to the local negotiators,
though in the exercise of it they must remember that similar
negotiations in other places will be affected by what they do.
Too great independence of action in one place may compromise
action already taken elsewhere in stricter conformity with the
words of the foregoing resolutions. No Communion, whether our
own or another, conducting negotiations in several places, will
consent to seriously divergent treatment of points which it counts
fundamental.

With these considerations in mind we offer suggestions on

one case, at the request of some of our number. Some Provinces of our Communion, while agreeing to unite with a non-episcopal Communion on the basis of the acceptance of Episcopacy for the future, might be faced with the necessity of providing for the contingency that many ministers who at the time of the union were working in the non-episcopal Communion, would remain after the union without episcopal ordination. The following suggestions appear to us to satisfy the conditions of local freedom explained above :—

(a) Ministers of both the uniting Communions should be at once recognized as of equal status in all Synods and Councils of the United Church.

(b) The terms of union should not confer on non-episcopally ordained ministers the right to administer the Holy Communion to those congregations which already possess an episcopal ministry, but they should include the right to conduct other services and to preach in such churches, if licensed thereto by the Bishop.

(c) All other matters might well be left to the decision of the Provincial or General Synods of the United Church, in full confidence that these Synods will take care not to endanger that fellowship with the universal Church which is our common ultimate aim.

The Committee asks the Conference to pass a Resolution of general approval of these suggestions.

Our brethren who have the responsibility of carrying through any such negotiations may be assured of our confidence in their loyalty, and of the support of the continuing prayer and sympathy which will follow them in their venture.

In concluding our Report we think it only right to state at the request of some of our number that, with regard to the precise phrasing and practical effect of some of the Resolutions which we have submitted to the Conference, there was considerable difference of opinion. They were finally accepted as representing the measure of general agreement which in the present circumstances we judged to be attainable in our Communion as a whole and on which alone counsel could fitly be based for the guidance of Bishops in the exercise of their own responsibility. But this very pressure of inevitable differences and difficulties called out among men widely sundered in opinion a spirit of patience, consideration, and unity for which we desire reverently to offer our thanksgiving to Him from Whom cometh down every good and perfect gift.

Part III.

Report of the Sub-Committee (a) on Relation to and Reunion with Episcopal Churches.

The Latin Communion.

Your Committee feels that it is impossible to make any Report on Reunion with Episcopal Churches without some reference to the Church of Rome, even though it has no resolution to propose upon the subject. We cannot do better than make our own the words of the Report of 1908, which reminds us of " the fact that there can be no fulfilment of the Divine purpose in any scheme of reunion which does not ultimately include the great Latin Church of the West, with which our history has been so closely associated in the past, and to which we are still bound by many ties of common faith and tradition." But we realize that—to continue the quotation—" any advance in this direction is at present barred by difficulties which we have not ourselves created, and which we cannot of ourselves remove." Should, however, the Church of Rome at any time desire to discuss conditions of reunion we shall be ready to welcome such discussions. We desire, moreover, very briefly to indicate that there are movements going on in the Church of Rome which may be fruitful in the future. There have been discussions in strict Roman Catholic circles in France as to the possibility of setting up an independent Gallican Church. The establishment of Houses of several of the Religious Orders at Oxford, and the part taken by their members in the discussions of theological societies there, together with their readiness to lecture at the " Summer School of Theology " which is entirely interdenominational, bear striking witness to the far greater freedom with which they enter into the intellectual life and interests of the Universities than formerly ; while the appearance of a work entitled " The Problem of Reunion," by a former Professor of Stonyhurst, is not without significance. A few years ago there would have been no " Problem " ; and though the writer maintains the traditional Roman position, he shews a marked difference, in tone and temperament, from what we have been accustomed to. They are also ready to join with us on a common platform in social and civic matters. Further, in spite of the official attitude taken by the Roman Church to our own with regard to religious ministrations during the war—an attitude which we greatly deplore—the personal relations, which obtained between their Chaplains and ours in France and elsewhere, were often of the pleasantest character and led to a greatly increased knowledge and understanding of each other's position It is obvious that no forward step can be taken yet ; but the facts thus referred to may help to create in the future a very different position

In what follows we desire to say how greatly we are indebted to the work of the last Lambeth Conference, and to the Reports of the several Committees appointed after its close Lines of advance in various directions were then laid down, and along these lines the Committees made real progress. It would have been quite impossible for us in the time at our disposal to fulfil the task imposed upon us had it not been for this We have for the most part taken up the work at the point at which they were compelled to leave it We have not attempted to go behind their conclusions, or examine afresh the evidence upon which they based them ; but, accepting them, we have worked upon them and have thus endeavoured to carry matters forward a stage nearer to the goal at which we are aiming

I

THE ORTHODOX EASTERN CHURCH.

We will begin by speaking about the Church of Russia. During the earlier years after the last Lambeth Conference our relations with this Church were probably closer than with any other branch of the Eastern Church, nor were they interfered with in the first years of the War, and after the Revolution in 1917 it was hoped that the internal reforms which the Russian Church—set free from State dominance, and adapting itself to the new conditions of life—was endeavouring to introduce, might bring about still closer relations with us This hope seemed to be confirmed by the fact that one of the last acts of the " Great Sobor " (Council) summoned by the Holy Synod was in September, 1918, to pass a resolution, welcoming " the sincere efforts of the Old Catholics and Anglicans towards union with the Orthodox Church," and calling on the sacred Synod " to organize a permanent commission with departments in Russia and abroad for the further study of Old Catholic and Anglican difficulties in the way of union, and for the furthering, as much as possible, of the speedy attainment of the final aim." Scarcely was this resolution passed before the Church in Russia was subjected to a renewed persecution, the horrors of which have hardly ever been exceeded. This is not the place to dwell on the martyrdoms of sixty bishops and hundreds of priests and other

L

persons. The memory of these things is in all our minds ; nor can we forget the way in which the Russian Church then turned to England, or the pathetic appeals addressed to the Archbishop of Canterbury for help and protection. The Conference will, we believe, desire to pass a resolution expressing its intense sympathy with the Russian Church in the terrible trials to which it has been and apparently still is being subjected. We therefore append one to this Report. Even now the position in Russia is far from clear. Information filters through but slowly. But one thing seems to stand out as certain, *viz.*, that in the wreck and ruin of all other institutions, the Church, albeit stripped and despoiled, alone has survived, though sorely hampered and hindered in the performance of its work, and we believe that when the opportunity for reconstructing its proper organization is given to it, it will once again look to establish the friendliest relations with the Anglican Church, relations which we trust and pray may be more intimate than ever.

With the Church of Serbia we must also express our deep sympathy, in view of the calamities and special difficulties which the War brought upon it. In its hour of trial it turned to England for help which was readily extended, and it has been a particular privilege for Church people in England to assist in the reconstruction of the Serbian Church. The entire body of Serbian students for Holy Orders were at one time receiving their education under the auspices of the Church of England at Oxford, Cuddesdon, and elsewhere, while every care was taken to maintain full loyalty to the Serbian Church Thus the closest relations were established between members of the two Churches, largely through the instrumentality of Father Nicholai Velimirovic, now Bishop of Zicha. At the present moment a number of Serbian students for Holy Orders are receiving their training in America, and the same cordial relationships are in existence there. These things mark a stage in the direction of reunion, the full results of which will be increasingly manifest in years to come.

In Greece also, and indeed in all parts of the East, the War has profoundly affected our relations with the Orthodox Church. It has brought the Anglican and Eastern Churches much nearer to each other. We hear from many different places of remarkable instances of what we may call informal acts of intercommunion in emergencies which would have been quite impossible a few years ago, and which shew the close sympathy there is between the two Churches. The War has changed the attitude of the East to Western Christendom. We are told that there is a great turning to England and America, and a desire to know more about us and our Communion, about which there is still too little known in the East generally. But partly because of the position of England in the War, and because of belief in its power, there has been a real stretching out of hands and a desire shewn in more than one quarter to learn and make advances towards us. It is well understood by this time in the East that we have no ulterior aims in seeking closer relations with them, and we are free from the suspicion of any attempt to proselytize, an attempt which naturally they would bitterly resent. During these last few years we have had several visits to our shores from distinguished Eastern prelates, and important Conferences have been held both in this country and in America for the discussion of doctrinal questions. We note also the cordial reception accorded to the Bishop of London and others in their visits to the East, and in particular the position assigned at the Liturgy to the Bishop of Gibraltar and the Bishop of Harrisburg, which seems to have gone beyond the extension of ordinary courtesies. These things will bear fruit in years to come. Another welcome sign of East and West drawing closer together is found in the letter from the *Locum tenens* of the Œcumenical Patriarchate at Constantinople " unto all the Churches of Christ wheresoever they be," which was sent from the Phanar to the Archbishop of Canterbury. Chief in importance, however, has been the visit of a special delegation from the Œcumenical Patriarchate to London, for purposes of consultation with Bishops attending the Lambeth Conference on relations between the Orthodox and Anglican Communions. This visit was the result of a formal invitation from the Archbishop of Canterbury to the *Locum tenens* of the Œcumenical Patriarchate at Constantinople. To this visit we have reason to attach the greatest importance. The delegation, consisting of Philaretos the Metropolitan of Demotica, Professor Komninos of Halki, the Archimandrite Pagonis of London, and the Archpriest Callinicos of Manchester, was welcomed by the President in full session of the Conference, and your Committee has had the advantage of more than one conference with it, at which important questions, doctrinal and practical, were discussed and full consideration given to the matters specified in the letter from the Phanar referred to above, in which letter we would call special attention to the desire expressed for immediate co-operation in matters of social reform.

Along the lines here briefly indicated we believe that we are steadily moving towards the goal of ultimate reunion. But there is much still to be done before this is reached, and our progress will be not less sure because it is slow. We still require to gain greater knowledge and understanding of each other's position. Explanations are needed on both sides, and it is clear that when the day comes for definite proposals of formal intercommunion to be made, they will have to be based on a large-hearted tolerance on both sides, and a readiness on the part of each Church to be content with holding its own uses and practices without attempting to ask for conformity to them on the part of the other.

Meanwhile, we look for much from the Eastern Churches' Committee recently appointed on a permanent basis by the Archbishop of Canterbury in pursuance of Resolution 61 of the last Lambeth Conference.　We are glad to learn that this action has been met by the appointment of somewhat similar Committees both at Constantinople and at Athens.　The American Church has also appointed a permanent Commission to confer with the Eastern Churches　We believe that through the action of these Committees further important steps towards reunion may be taken, partly by the free discussion of doctrinal matters, e g., the meaning of the Filioque clause, as not involving any belief on our part in more than one αἰτία in the Godhead, our doctrine of holy orders, the position of the XXXIX Articles, on all of which matters the Easterns are asking for information, and partly also by conference on practical matters of moment, such as the better regulation of mixed marriages, the reciprocal administration of the Sacraments in cases of emergency, a uniform Kalendar, possibly involving the appointment of a fixed Easter, and other questions raised in the letter from the Phanar.

We need at the present time not only or chiefly to afford to the Easterns historical evidence of the handing down of our ministry, but also to explain the doctrinal position held by our Communion. It is in particular of the first importance, in order to remove Oriental misconceptions, to make it clear from our formularies that we regard Ordination as conferring grace, and not only as a mere setting apart to an ecclesiastical office.　It would also (though in a lesser degree) be a help, as well as a good thing in itself, to restore the true text of the " Nicene " Creed, as it is used in all parts of the East and West, except in our Communion, by replacing the word " Holy " before " Catholic and Apostolic Church."

If some members of the Eastern Churches' Committee could visit Athens or Constantinople for conferences to be held there, such as those already held in this country and in America, we believe that they would not only meet with a cordial welcome, but also be able to do much to remove misconceptions, and to prepare the way for the ultimate reunion which both Churches alike so earnestly desire, and for which they make their constant prayer.

II.

The Separated Churches of the East.

Since the last Lambeth Conference further steps have been taken towards a better understanding of, and in some cases a nearer relation to, those Ancient Churches of the East which by reason mainly of the Christological dissensions of the Fifth century have been separated from the rest of Christianity. But the persecutions which many of them, notably the Armenians, Nestorians, and Syrian Jacobites, have been called upon to suffer, both before and during the Great War, and the terrible massacres that have taken place among them, have prevented as great progress being made as might have been hoped. That they have so greatly suffered for the Christian faith and have refused to apostatize from it under persecution is a fact which must call for our deepest sympathy and respect.

These Churches have all at some period of their history been accused of theological error with regard to the Incarnation, and it is, therefore, necessary that we should examine with some care their doctrinal position at the present time. The Lambeth Conference of 1908 desired the formation of Commissions to do this, and "to prepare some carefully framed statement of the faith as to our Lord's Person, in the simplest possible terms, which should be submitted to each of such Churches where feasible, in order to ascertain whether it represents their belief with substantial accuracy." Further, the Conference suggested that if such a statement were found to be acceptable to any such Church occasional intercommunion might be advantageously provided for. A Commission was formed, and proceeded to take action with reference to the *East Syrian, Assyrian*, or *Nestorian Church ;* and it resolved that the statement of Catholic doctrine to be submitted to this Church, or to any other that lay under analogous suspicion of error as to the Incarnation, should be the Christological versicles of the Quicunque Vult. The Commission also resolved to ask the East Syrian Church to explain in what sense it used the term " Mother of Christ " as its technical description of the Blessed Virgin Mary. The Archbishop of Canterbury wrote to this effect to the now deceased Patriarch Benjamin Mar Shimun, Catholicos of the East, who, after consultation with his bishops, and with their assent, returned answer under date June 13th, 1911, entirely accepting the statement of faith propounded to him, as expressing the belief of that Church, and giving an explanation of the use of the term " Mother of Christ " which was considered entirely satisfactory by the Commission. With this judgement your present Committee agree.

It was, however, more important still that a careful examination of the East Syrian voluminous liturgical books should be made. This has been done, with the result that it is seen that they contain much that is incompatible with real Nestorianism, together with some things that might be interpreted either in an orthodox or in a Nestorian sense ; it is suggested that the latter must be judged by the former. The watchword Theotokos is absent from their service books, and in one place is repudiated ;

on the other hand, its equivalent in other words is several times found, and strong instances of the language known as *communicatio idiomatum* occur One phrase, which has caused some perplexity, is that which asserts that there are in Christ one parsōpā (πρόσωπον), two Qnōmé, and two natures. The word Qnōmā is equivalent to "hypostasis," and if used in the later sense of that word, *i e.* as meaning "person," it would imply real Nestorianism , but research has made it plain that it is used in the earlier sense of "hypostasis," namely, "substance," and this makes the phrase, if redundant, at least perfectly orthodox. It should be added that the East Syrians accept the decrees of Chalcedon, while rejecting those of Ephesus.

Your Committee agree with the Commission in thinking that we need not insist on the East Syrian Church ceasing to mention in their services the names of those whom it has hitherto revered.

They suggest that if the Archbishop of Canterbury finds that the present East Syrian authorities adhere to the answer given in 1911, there is no reason why occasional intercommunion should not be established. They also think that opportunity should be taken to inform the authorities of the Eastern Orthodox Churches about these proposals.

The Jacobites or West Syrians.—Since the last Lambeth Conference the Jacobite Patriarch, Mar Ignatius Abdullah II, has visited this country His interview with the late Bishop of Salisbury (Dr J Wordsworth) at the end of 1908 gives us much information as to the doctrinal position of his Church ; in particular he called attention to the *Statement of Faith*, or Creed, of which an English translation was published by the Syrian Patriarchate Education Committee in 1908, and by Dr. Wordsworth in 1909, as being a very ancient and authoritative document by which his Church was solemnly bound. This *Statement of Faith* denies that the divine nature of our Lord was commingled with the human nature, or that the two natures became commixed and changed so as to give rise to a third nature, and asserts that the two natures became united in indissoluble union without confusion, mixture, or transmutation, and that they remained two natures in an unalterable unity (§ 12). The *Statement of Faith* is quite free from Monophysitism, and contains the emphatic assertion that the Trisagion as recited by the Jacobites, with the addition of " who wast crucified for us "—an addition long looked on as a strong mark of error—is addressed, not to the Holy Trinity, but solely " to the only-begotten Son, the Word, who was pleased to be born of the Holy Virgin Mary and became flesh " (§ 22).

Your Committee regretfully recognize that the present moment, when under the draft Turkish Treaty the West Syrians remain under Turkish rule, is not specially suitable for endeavouring to establish closer relations with them ; but suggest that the recently appointed Eastern Churches Committee should watch for any suitable opportunity for doing so, and that when such opportunity arises, the above considerations will greatly diminish any doctrinal difficulties. In the meantime a great desideratum is a better knowledge of the Jacobite liturgical books, which are mostly in manuscript

Copts and Abyssinians.—The above-mentioned Patriarch, Mar Ignatius Abdullah, stated that there is free intercourse between West Syrians, Armenians, Copts, and Abyssinians. In view of this fact any problems as to nearer relations between them and ourselves would be greatly simplified At any moment opportunities of closer official relations with the Copts may arise, and in view of them your Committee suggest the desirability of a more thorough examination of their service books than has yet been made.

The Armenians.—This great and much-suffering Church has always repudiated charges of Eutychianism or of Monophysitism, and it is probable that their refusal to accept the decrees of Chalcedon is due to their having been prevented by political causes from being present at that Council, and to its decisions having reached them in a faulty version. Your Committee would express the hope that by the speedy development of mutual intercourse and investigation, closer relations may be established between them and ourselves, and that the Eastern Churches Committee should be asked to take notice of any suitable opportunity in this direction

The Christians of St. Thomas in Malabar.—In so far as these Christians give allegiance to the West or East Syrians, the remarks made about those Churches apply here. In another part of this report reference is made to a large scheme of reunion which is being discussed in Southern India, and is intended to include some at least of these Christians.

Your Committee would suggest that it is not necessary, even if it were possible, to determine how far the Separated Churches of the East have been in the past really implicated in the errors which have been attributed to them, but they think that the investigations of the last twelve years have gone a great way to shew that they have at any rate grown out of any errors they may have held on the Person and Natures of our Lord. The more this is made clear, the more it will appear to be possible to arrive at occasional intercommunion, at the least. But it is desirable that an endeavour should be made, as we move forward step by step in this direction, to explain our attitude carefully to the authorities of the Orthodox Eastern Church, that all misconceptions with regard to the subject on the part of that great Communion may be removed Indeed, we have good reason to believe that such action as is here indicated would in no ways prejudice our relations with the Orthodox.

III.

THE CHURCH OF SWEDEN

In consequence of Resolution 74 of the last Lambeth Conference a Commission was appointed by the Archbishop of Canterbury in 1909 under the chairmanship of the Bishop of Winchester (Dr. Ryle) to correspond with the Swedish Church on the possibility suggested by the Archbishop of Upsala (Dr. Ekman) of an " alliance of some sort " between the Swedish and Anglican Churches. In the autumn of the same year the Commission visited Sweden and held an important Conference with distinguished representatives of the Swedish Church At this Conference explanations were given with regard to the Episcopal succession in both countries and with regard to other matters which required elucidation, and a Committee was appointed by the Archbishop of Upsala to act with him for the purpose of continuing if necessary the discussions initiated in the Conference. In the following year Bishop John Wordsworth delivered his memorable " Hale Lectures " (published in 1911) on " The National Church of Sweden." In the same year was also published a learned work by another member of the Anglican Commission, *viz*, Bishop Mott Williams (then Bishop of Marquette), on " The Church of Sweden and the Anglican Communion." These two volumes dealt fully with the question of the succession of Swedish orders, and did much to remove the doubts previously felt on this subject in some quarters. In the course of the next year (1911) the Archbishop's Commission made its formal report, in which it stated the following conclusions, arrived at after full consideration of the evidence laid before it :—
" (1) That the succession of bishops has been maintained unbroken by the Church of Sweden, and that it has a true conception of the episcopal office . . . and (2) that the office of priest is also rightly conceived as a divinely instituted instrument for the ministry of Word and Sacraments, and that it has been in intention handed on throughout the whole history of the Church of Sweden "

Accepting these conclusions, they based on them a recommendation that a resolution should be proposed, similar to that which was adopted by the Lambeth Conference of 1888 in reference to the Old Catholics of Germany, Austria, and Switzerland, under which members of the National Church of Sweden, otherwise qualified to receive the Sacrament in their own Church, might be admitted to Communion in ours. They also suggested that " permission might with advantage occasionally be given to Swedish ecclesiastics to give addresses in our churches," and that " notice should be sent to the Archbishop of Upsala of important events or appointments within the Church of England,

and that we should welcome similar information on his part "—
a suggestion which, we understand, has been already to some
extent acted upon. Further, they said that "as regards
facilities for the use of churches for marriages, burials, and the
like where Swedish churches are not available, we believe that
concession on this head is within the competence of any diocesan
bishop, and we trust that such facilities may be generally
granted."

We accept the conclusions arrived at by the learned men who
formed this Commission, on the unbroken succession of the Episcopate in Sweden, and on the conception of the office of priest held by
that Church ; and we recommend to the Conference the adoption
of the definite recommendations cited above. We also hold
that the time has come when, in the event of an invitation to
an Anglican bishop or bishops to take part in the consecration
of a Swedish bishop, it might properly be accepted. Such an
invitation was, we understand, actually made in the year 1914,
but it was then thought that the time had not come for such
action, as the Report of the Commission had not been then
before the Lambeth Conference. This reason no longer exists,
and in the event of our resolutions based on this Report being
approved, we believe that there need be hesitation no longer.
Only we would add the recommendation that the acceptance of
any such invitation should be subject to the approval of the
Metropolitan of the Province, so that the invitation might be
considered as one made from Church to Church, and not simply
as a personal matter. We think also that in the first instance,
as an evident token of the restoration of close relations between
the two Churches, it is desirable that more than one of our bishops
should take part in the action.

We ought not to conclude this section of our Report without
stating that we are fully aware that in regard to the Diaconate
and the administration of Confirmation the Swedish Church
does not conform to the practice required within the Anglican
Communion. But we have come to the conclusion that this
fact ought not to be allowed to be a bar to such more intimate
relations as we recommend. We express a hope, however, that
as a result of the closer intimacy which we desire to be established,
an intimacy which is happily encouraged and fostered by the
presence of many Swedish students in this country, the Swedish
Church may be led to consider the restoration of the Diaconate,
and also of the laying-on of hands as an outward sign of grace
given in Confirmation.*

* The subjects of the diaconate and Confirmation were considered at
the Conference at Upsala in 1909. See the *Report of the Commission*,
pp 10, 11. Reference may also be made to Bishop Wordsworth's *Hale
Lectures*, pp. 351–55, and 417–18, and Bishop Mott Williams' *The Church
of Sweden and the Anglican Communion*, pp 66–81.

We have said nothing in this Report of the other Scandinavian Churches, *viz.* those of Denmark, Norway, and Finland; not from any lack of sympathy or of desire for closer relations with them, but because the problem in their case is different from that in the case of the Church of Sweden, and because we believe that the time has not yet come for such negotiations to be entered into with them as are now proceeding with the Swedish Church. We hold, therefore, that at present it is wise to be content with aiming at closer alliance with the last-named Church alone.

IV.

THE OLD CATHOLICS.

The "friendly relations" with the Old Catholics referred to in Resolution 68 of the last Lambeth Conference were steadily carried on, until the outbreak of the War in 1914 rendered communications and intercourse with them very difficult, and in some places quite impossible. Even now, although hostilities have ceased for more than a year and a half, the disturbed and unsettled condition of a large part of Europe remains a great hindrance to intercourse. We look forward, however, hopefully to a resumption in the near future of such happy relations as existed before the war, and it is a hopeful sign that the Old Catholic Bishops have quite recently been able for the first time for several years to meet together in Conference. Mention should also be made here of the remarkable rise of the Mariaviten Church in Poland, which has naturally suffered greatly during the War, and of the recent movement for reforms of various kinds within the Roman Catholic Church in Czecho-Slovakia, a movement the course of which we shall watch with interest.

In Resolution 69 of 1908 the Conference deprecated " the setting up of a new organised body in regions where a Church with apostolic ministry and Catholic doctrine offers religious privileges without the imposition of uncatholic terms of communion." The occasion which called forth this resolution was the consecration, at Utrecht on April 28th, 1908, of the Rev. A. H. Mathew by the Old Catholic Bishops for work in this country; and the resolution was at the request of the Conference communicated to the Archbishop of Utrecht by the Archbishop of Canterbury. Your Committee note with thankfulness that, in reply to this, explanations were offered by the Archbishop of Utrecht, and a promise made that in future they " would take care not to make trouble by encroaching on the order of a friendly Church." This statement has quite recently been followed up by a formal pronouncement by the Old Catholic

Bishops assembled at Utrecht on April 28th and 29th, 1920, in which they state categorically that the episcopal consecration of the Rev A. H. Mathew " was surreptitiously secured by the production of false testimony, and would never have taken place had the consecrators known that the conditions stated in the questionable documents and required by our Episcopate were non-existent." They also state that on the discovery of the facts they " broke off intercourse with him," and " without entering on the question whether an ordination obtained by sacrilegious fraud can be valid " declare that they " have no ecclesiastical relations " with those persons who claim to have received ordination or consecration from the aforesaid person. In these circumstances your Committee have had to consider most carefully what should be the attitude of the Anglican Communion to those persons who claim to exercise priestly or episcopal functions with a succession derived from Bishop Mathew personally, or from those who claim to be his successors in the Episcopate ; and on a review of all the facts they are driven to the conclusion that it is not possible to regard the so-called " Old Catholic Church in Great Britain," disclaimed as it is by the Old Catholics on the Continent, as a properly constituted branch of the Church, or to recognize the orders of its ministers. The circumstances of Bishop Mathew's consecration are so uncertain, and his subsequent isolation is so complete, that, without casting any sort of reflection on the validity of Old Catholic orders, or discussing the theological question of abstract " validity," we feel that as a matter of practice, in the event of any persons ordained by him or by his successors desiring to come over to the Anglican Church, and exercise their ministry in communion with it, the only proper course would be for them (if in all respects suitable) to be ordained *sub conditione*.* We recommend therefore that this course should be followed, and that, in order to make the position perfectly clear, the condition should be definitely stated in a document subscribed both by the Bishop ordaining and by the person to be ordained, and further that it should be expressed in the Letters of Orders, somewhat after the precedent set by Archbishop Bramhall in the case of some Presbyterians ordained by him in the Seventeenth century.†

* A Memorandum on " Conditional Ordination " was prepared by the Bishop of Gloucester for the use of the Conference, and will shortly be published

† The following is the form used by Bramhall :—" Non annihilantes priores ordines (si quos habuit) nec invaliditatem eorundem determinantes, multo minus omnes ordines sacros ecclesiarum forinsecarum condemnantes, quos proprio Judici relinquimus, sed solummodo supplentes quicquid prius defuit per canones ecclesiæ Anglicanæ requisitum, et providentes paci ecclesiæ,§ut schismatis tollatur occasio, et conscientiis fidelium satisfiat nec ulli dubitent de ejus ordinatione, aut actus suos presbyteriales tanquam invalidos_aversentur."—Bramhall's *Works*, vol. i., p 37.

A similar course we recommend to be followed in the case of persons ordained by Bishop Vernon Herford, " Bishop of Mercia " (who claims to have received consecration from " Mar Basilius, Metropolitan of India, &c "), or by other " episcopi vagantes," whose consecration and status we are unable to recognize. But before action is taken in this way by any individual Bishop we recommend that, after he has satisfied himself that the case is one in which it is desirable to proceed (a most necessary precaution), he should consult the Metropolitan of the Province, and place the case fully before him.

V.

THE *UNITAS FRATRUM* OR MORAVIANS.

The question of the position of the Moravians was first referred to in the Lambeth Conference so far back as 1878, but nothing of importance was done until in 1897 the Conference passed the two following resolutions :—" 37. That this Conference, not possessing sufficient information to warrant the expression of a decided opinion upon the question of the orders of the *Unitas Fratrum* or Moravians, must content itself with expressing a hearty desire for such relations with them as will aid the cause of Christian Unity, and with recommending that there should be on the part of the Anglican Communion further consideration of the whole subject, in the hope of establishing closer relations between the *Unitas Fratrum* and the Churches represented in this Conference " " 38. That the Archbishop of Canterbury be requested to appoint a Committee to conduct the further investigation of the subject, and for such purpose to confer with the authorities or representatives of the *Unitas Fratrum.*" In accordance with this resolution a Committee was appointed in 1906 by the Archbishop of Canterbury which entered on a thorough investigation of the question of the succession of Moravian Bishops, the result of which was that in their opinion, though " a succession of regularly constituted ministers has beyond question been maintained in that community from the year 1467 to the present time," it is " a matter of grave doubt whether the ministry so maintained is in the strict sense an episcopal ministry." The Committee, which issued its Report in 1907, most regretfully arrived at this conclusion, viz. that " the way to immediate intercommunion with the Unity as a Sister Church seems to be at present barred by the great uncertainty of its possessing the historic Episcopate." This conclusion was received with great disappointment by the authorities of the Moravians, who, as was perhaps natural, could not agree with the verdict on the historical question, but frankly recognized that any further negotiations on the part of the Anglican Church could only be carried on on the basis of that Report. They were, however, desirous that the next Lambeth Conference might take the matter up again, and asked that we should consider the possibility of such participation on our side in Moravian consecrations as would put Moravian orders for the future into a position satisfactory to Anglicans. Accordingly the matter came up again at the Conference of 1908 ; and the following resolutions were adopted :—

" 70. For the sake of unity, and as a particular expression of brotherly affection, we recommend that any official request of the *Unitas Fratrum* for the participation of Anglican Bishops in the consecration of Bishops of the *Unitas* should be accepted, provided that

" (i) Such Anglican Bishops should be not less than three in number, and should participate both in the saying of the Prayers of Consecration and in the laying on of hands, and that the rite itself is judged to be sufficient by the Bishops of the Church of our Communion to which the invited Bishops belong ,

" (ii) The Synods of the *Unitas* (a) are able to give sufficient assurance of doctrinal agreement with ourselves in all essentials (as we believe that they will be willing and able to do) , and (b) are willing to explain its position as that of a religious community or missionary body in close alliance with the Anglican Communion ; and (c) are willing to accord a due recognition to the position of our Bishops within Anglican Dioceses and jurisdictions ; and (d) are willing to adopt a rule as to the administration of Confirmation more akin to our own.

" 71. After the conditions prescribed in the preceding Resolution have been complied with, and a Bishop has been consecrated in accordance with them, corresponding invitations from any Bishop of the *Unitas Fratrum* to an Anglican Bishop and his Presbyters to participate in the Ordination of a Moravian Presbyter should be accepted, provided that the Anglican Bishop should participate both in the saying of the Prayers of Ordination and in the laying-on of hands, and that the rite itself is judged to be sufficient by the Bishops of the Church of our Communion to which the invited Bishop belongs.

" 72. Any Bishop or Presbyter so consecrated or ordained should be free to minister in the Anglican Communion with due episcopal licence ; and, in the event of the above proposals, *i.e.* Resolutions 1 and 2, being accepted and acted upon by the Synods of the *Unitas*, during the period of transition some permission to preach in our churches might on special occasions be extended to Moravian Ministers by Bishops of our Communion

" 73. We recommend that the Archbishop of Canterbury be respectfully requested to name a Committee to communicate, as need arises, with representatives of the *Unitas*, and also to direct that the decisions of the present Conference be communicated to the *Secretarius Unitatis*."

This last resolution was promptly carried out. A Committee was appointed under the chairmanship of the Bishop of Durham (Dr. Moule) and negotiations were entered upon with the *Unitas*. The course of these negotiations and the explanations offered by the Moravians are fully described in the Report of the Committee which was prepared in 1913, and in which they state that the "conditions contained in Resolution 70 (i) and (ii) have now been satisfied." Since then, however, questions have arisen as to the completeness of the fulfilment of the conditions on the part of the *Unitas*, especially in regard to provisions (*b*) and (*c*), and even more in regard to (*d*), as it now appears that the *Unitas* permits deacons to celebrate Holy Communion, and also to administer Confirmation. This fact was unknown to the Committee when it made its report early in 1913. Since then the subject has been on two occasions brought before the Central Consultative Body of the Lambeth Conference (in July, 1913, and again in 1914), and that body came to the conclusion that it "did not feel itself justified in saying that in its judgement the conditions laid down in 70 (ii) of the Lambeth Conference have been so completely and satisfactorily met as to enable the participating action to be carried out," and it "recommended that the full Lambeth Conference at its next meeting should have an opportunity of expressing its opinion." From this time till now negotiations have been practically in abeyance, though quite recently informal communications have taken place between one or more members of the Committee and the Moravians. In these circumstances your Committee has had to consider the matter most carefully, and we have been greatly helped by a conference with Bishop Mumford, the President of the Provincial Board of the Moravian Church in Great Britain and Ireland. The time at our disposal has been too short for us to go into the questions at issue as fully as we would wish to have done. We are agreed, however, that condition (*a*) in 70 (ii) is satisfied ; but there is still some uncertainty as to (*b*) and (*c*) ; and it is in our opinion impossible for any such action to take place as is contemplated in the resolution so long as the present practice of the Moravians in regard to the celebration of the Holy Communion and the administration of Confirmation by deacons remains unchanged. It might be possible, we think, for the fact of Confirmation by a Presbyter to be regarded as no bar to the measure of intercommunion proposed, provided that it were distinctly laid down that authority for such action on the part of Presbyters was directly delegated to them by the Bishop, there being precedents for this both in East and West. And if the *Unitas Fratrum* can see its way to meet our requirements in these matters we think that negotiations with them might well be resumed, and we hope that the result would be that any remaining uncertainty as to 70 (ii) (*b*) and (*c*) would be removed. Should this happy consummation be arrived at we believe that they might then, through the Archbishop of Canterbury, invite Anglican Bishops to participate in a consecration without fear of refusal. The existing difficulties have already been brought before the authorities of the *Unitas*, and we are encouraged by statements made to us to hope that such a change of rule on its part is not out of the question. We therefore suggest that the Committee appointed after the last Lambeth Conference should be continued in existence, and strengthened by the addition of two members to supply the place of the late Bishop of Durham and Bishop Mitchinson ; and that this Committee should be ready, whenever the proper time comes, to re-enter upon negotiations with the *Unitas* ; and we further recommend that if the difficulties described above can be removed to the satisfaction of the Archbishop of Canterbury with the concurrence of the Consultative Body, there would then be no need to wait for another Lambeth Conference before action was taken It should be added that in making these recommendations we have directly in view only the branch of the *Unitas Fratrum* in the British Isles. We are given to understand that as " a full Province " it has complete liberty to act by itself in this matter. But if the negotiations with the *Unitas* in the British Province can be carried to a successful issue, a valuable precedent will have been set, which may well be followed in other Provinces, and thus lead ultimately to complete intercommunion between the Anglican Communion and the *Unitas* in all parts of the world.

VI.

" THE REFORMED EPISCOPAL CHURCH."

This body has now about twenty-five congregations or churches in England served by thirty or forty ministers. It was introduced into this country from America, where it originated in 1866, and where there are still a certain number of its congregations. We are called on to consider it here because its " Southern Synod " has passed " by a large majority," and forwarded to the authorities of the English Church, the following resolution :—

" This Synod, being desirous, so far as in it lies, of maintaining unity among all Christian people, would be prepared to consider the question of the Union of the Reformed Episcopal Church with the Established Church of England, provided that the ministers of the Reformed Episcopal Church are received as clergy duly ordained in accordance with the Articles of that Church, and that it is allowed to retain its Declaration of Principles unaltered with its Doctrine, Discipline, and Worship, as set forth in its Constitution, Canons, and Prayer Book."

Less formal proposals of a somewhat different character have also been received, suggesting that " the clergy should be re-ordained by the Anglican Bishops (or by one Bishop acting for the rest) and be permitted to minister to the congregations that they are at present serving, and that the congregations should be admitted to union with the Church of England under the provisions of an approved trust deed, which would secure the maintenance of the Evangelical character of their work "

Your Committee has had before it full particulars not only of the organization, worship, and principles of this body, but also of the origin of its ministry, and its claim to an Episcopal succession.* The members of the Committee find themselves quite unable to recommend the Conference to accept that claim. On this ground, therefore, they are compelled to recommend the Conference to decline to enter into negotiations with the Synod on the basis of the proposals made by it. With regard to the less formal proposal, they feel it necessary to point out that evidence has been before them that the standard of qualifications for the ministry in the Reformed Episcopal Church is such that it would not be easy for us to take any action with regard to the body corporately Difficulties would arise in individual cases which in so small a body might assume serious proportions.   There are also matters such as the nature of their trust deeds and the character of their Prayer Book, which might easily lead to complications. We think therefore that it is not desirable to enter into negotiations with the body as a whole But, as the experience of the last few years has shewn that a tendency exists in both ministers and congregations of the Reformed Episcopal Church to apply for reunion with the Church of England, we recommend that such applications should be, wherever possible, sympathetically treated, and that if the minister satisfies our standards intellectually as well as in other ways, he should be ordained *sub conditione* ; and that if the practical difficulties in the way of

* The origin of the Reformed Episcopal Church is explained in " A Statement in regard to Ordinations or Consecrations performed by Dr. Cummins, or others claiming Ordination or Consecration from him, prepared by the Presiding Bishop of the American Church, the Right Rev John Williams, D D ,LL D ," which was submitted to the Lambeth Conference of 1888. The chief facts stated in this document are apparently not denied, though the conclusions drawn from them are traversed in *The Origin, Orders, Organisation, and Worship of the Reformed Episcopal Church in the United Kingdom*, by Philip X. Eldridge, D.D., Presiding Bishop (1910).

congregations joining us can be overcome they should be received
on the condition that as loyal English Church people they accept
the Book of Common Prayer in place of the book now in use
in the Reformed Episcopal Church.

Part IV.

Conclusion.

It is impossible for those who have worked point by point
over the difficult ground covered by this Report to judge what
impression it will make upon those who come to it freshly and
as a whole. Some will probably find in it at some points laxity
in the enforcement of principle: others may charge it with
rigidity.

To some it will seem to move too rashly: others will com-
plain that it moves so little. Yet most earnestly do we hope
that there may be real value found in what has been arrived at
with so large a measure of unity, and with a sense of constraint
towards agreement which surprised ourselves, and seemed, as we
reverently believe, to be of the Spirit's guidance.

The wounds of the Church of Christ are very deep and very
stiff with time and controversy

They cannot be quickly healed. Rather will they have to
be first more deeply probed, and the measure of the contrast
between men's doings and God's purpose more fully understood.
Certainly the sense of being drawn together and drawn upward
was never so strong or so uplifting as when we were moved to
look beyond smaller ideals and limited agreements to the vision
of the One Holy Catholic Church of the Divine Redeemer, into
which all the ivided groups of His faithful people must bring
what they have of glory and honour, and which cannot be made
perfect till all its parts are drawn together in Him. If there is
any value in this Report it comes from the inspiration of that
only true and divine ideal.

(Signed)   COSMO EBOR:

Chairman.

Ingram Content Group UK Ltd.
Milton Keynes UK
UKHW020654240323
419106UK00007B/579